access to philosophy

THE THEORY *of* KNOWLEDGE

Peter Cole

Acknowledgements

Cover photo from Mary Evans Picture Library by Walter Molino (1955) for the publication 'La Domenica del Corriere'.

The publishers would like to thank the following companies for permission to reproduce copyright illustrations in this book:

The Kobal Collection, page 8; Bettman/Corbis, page 19, AKG London/ Erich Lessing, page 52.

The publishers would also like to thank the following for permission to reproduce material in this book:

Routledge for extracts from *An Introduction to Philosophical Analysis* by J Hospers, 1997; Blackwell Publishing Ltd for extracts from *An Introduction to the Philosophy of the Mind* by K Maslin, Polity Press, 2001 and *An Introduction to Epistemology* by C Landesman, Blackwell, 1997; Edinburgh University Press for extracts from *God, Reason and Theistic Proofs* by Stephen Davis, 1997; Oxford University Press (New York) for extracts from *Descartes* by G Dicker, 1993; Oxford University Press (UK) for extracts from *The Rationalists* by John Cottingham, 1998, *David Hume: An Enquiry Concerning Human Understanding* edited by Tom L. Beauchamp, Oxford Philosophical Texts, 1999, and *The Empiricists* by R S Woolhouse, 1988; Everyman Publishers Plc for extracts from *Meditation 2*, by Descartes and *Essay Concerning Human Understanding* by John Locke.

Every effort has been made to trace and acknowledge ownership of copyright. The publishers will be glad to make suitable arrangements with any copyright holders whom it has not been possible to contact.

Orders: Please contact Bookpoint Ltd, 130 Milton Park, Abingdon, Oxon OX14 4SB. Telephone: (44) 01235 827720. Fax: (44) 01235 400454. Lines are open from 9.00am - 5.00pm Monday to Saturday, with a 24-hour message answering service. You can also order through our website at www.hoddereducation.co.uk

British Library Cataloguing in Publication Data
A catalogue for this title is available from The British Library

ISBN-13: 978 0 340 80482 7

First published 2002
Impression number   10   9   8   7
Year   2008

Typeset by Transet Limited, Coventry, England
Printed in Great Britain for Hodder Education, part of Hachette Livre UK, 338 Euston Road, London NW1 3BH by CPI Antony Rowe

Contents

	Preface	v
Chapter 1	Assumptions, Reasoning and Arguments	1
	1 Introduction	1
	2 Assumptions	2
	3 Reasoning	3
	4 Alternatives	5
	Study guides	5
Chapter 2	Knowledge	7
	1 What is real?	7
	2 Epistemology	9
	3 Knowledge	11
	Study guides	15
Chapter 3	Rationalism	17
	1 Rationalism	17
	2 Descartes	19
	3 Descartes' arguments	20
	4 Weaknesses of rationalism	23
	5 The limits of rationalism	24
	Study guides	25
Chapter 4	Empiricism	27
	1 What is empiricism?	27
	2 Differences beween empiricism and rationalism	28
	3 The empiricists' argument	28
	4 Challenges to Locke	29
	5 Hume's empiricism	30
	6 The limits of empiricism	30
	7 Kant's synthesis	30
	8 Criticisms of Kant	33
	Study guides	35
Chapter 5	Scepticism	37
	1 What is scepticism?	37
	2 Brief history of scepticism	37
	3 Reasons for scepticism	38
	4 Types of doubt	39
	5 The merits of philosophical doubt	39
	6 Is total scepticism possible?	40
	Study guides	42

Chapter 6 Justification 43
    I What is justification? 43
    2 Theories of justification 44
    Study guides 48

Chapter 7 Theories of truth 50
    I Truth 50
    2 The correspondence theory 51
    3 The coherency theory 53
    4 The pragmatic theory 54
    5 More recent approaches 54
    Study guides 55

Chapter 8 The problem of perception 56
    I The problem 56
    2 Primary and secondary qualities 57
    3 Descartes' wax illustration 58
    4 Naïve realism 59
    5 Representative realism 60
    6 Idealism 61
    7 Phenomenalism 63
    Study guides 64

Chapter 9 The scope of knowledge 65
    I The external world 65
    2 The past 72
    3 The future 73
    Study guides 76

Chapter 10 Descartes' *Meditations*
    (an appendix on Cartesian dualism) 77
    I The 'I' 78
    2 Arguments for the material world 78
    3 Arguments for Cartesian dualism 79
    4 Interactionism 80
    5 Problems with interactionism 81
    6 Descartes' contribution 83
    Study guides 84

    Further reading 85

    Index 86

Preface

To the reader

Access books are written mainly for students studying for examinations at higher level, particularly GCE Advanced Subsidiary (AS) level and Advanced (A) level, the Scottish National Qualifications in RMPS at Intermediate 2 and Higher Levels as well as the IB examinations.

To use this book most effectively, you should be aware of the following features.

- The Contents list gives a breakdown of the main sections in each chapter.
- Within each chapter, the material is broken down into subheadings and bullet points to make it easier to use.
- The Key Words at the beginning of each chapter are for easy reference and to help you become more familiar with the technical language of the subject.
- There are suggestions for further reading at the end of each chapter.
- There are also Summary lists of the main points at the end of each section. It can form the outline of your study notes on the topic. It is also a quick revision tool.
- There is also help with answering examination questions, and a list of typical questions is given. Do tackle the specimen questions, just planning your answers to some of them and writing others in full.

General advice on answering essay questions

Structured questions will tell you what to include.

- Make sure that you are aware of the number of marks available for each part question, and plan your time accordingly, so that you spend more time on the parts for which more marks are available.
- Before you choose your questions, make sure that you have read both parts and are confident about both.
- The first part of the question is aimed to assess your knowledge and understanding of the topic, and your skills in presenting a description. Try to keep to what is relevant, and use technical terms correctly where you can. Aim to provide some evidence of your background reading, by referring to the author or the title of the book, or by contrasting one thinker with another.
- The second part is designed to assess your evaluative skills. This is not the place to present a lot more description, but to weigh the evidence. Often, these questions consist of a statement followed by 'Discuss.' Try and explain why some people would agree with the statement, while others disagree. Aim to give supported reasons for your own position, rather than just saying 'I feel' without any justification.

1 Assumptions, Reasoning and Arguments

KEY ISSUE How philosophy opens up new ideas and possibilities – things never considered before – by challenging assumptions and using reasoning.

1 Introduction

I am sitting with a philosopher in the garden:
he says again and again 'I know that that is a tree',
pointing to a tree that is near us.
Someone else arrives and hears this,
and I tell him. 'This fellow isn't insane.
We are only doing philosophy.'

L Wittgenstein, 1951

The popular image of a philosopher is of someone rather vague and dreamy who worries about whether or not the chair is really there. The implication is that philosophers do not live in the real world and they worry about things that are obvious to any sane person.

Philosophers are seen as irrelevant – people who don't contribute to knowledge or life in any significant way, and who spend their lives asking pointless questions.

Students of philosophy can find the subject frustrating because it never seems to provide any answers. Indeed the same questions seem to have been discussed throughout the centuries but without a resolution. Paradoxically, students are often confronted with a wide choice of answers rather than no answers at all, which adds to the sense of frustration. This makes choice even more difficult. In addition, the answers include some radical alternatives that students hadn't considered before. Philosophy dares to think the unthinkable. That is both its fascination and frustration.

Philosophers do worry how they know whether the chair is there or not. But the answer 'It's obvious' is not an answer that is satisfactory. Philosophy makes us uncomfortable because it dares to question 'common sense'. This is because it assumes no necessary connection between 'common sense' and 'truth'. It assumes nothing and tries to root out all assumptions in order to challenge them. We do this not to be obtuse but to be clear in our reasoning. Philosophy asks difficult questions about the world around us and about our experiences. It asks one of the most difficult questions of all: What is the basis of our knowledge? How do we know anything?

This question about knowledge and how we know things is the issue at the heart of this book. In philosophy we call this study **epistemology**.

Before we look at the topic in detail, it may be worthwhile reviewing the approach that philosophy demands – the very things that cause frustration to many students of this discipline.

2 Assumptions

Task: Plant four trees in a garden so that each tree is equidistant from each of the other trees.

If you give someone a piece of paper and ask them to mark the place where the trees should be planted they will not find it easy. Most will put them in a square and then realise that the diagonal is longer than the side. Others will put them in a circle only to realise that the trees really just form a square and so, again, are not an equal distance apart. Many will decide that the task cannot be done because there is no logical solution.

The solution in fact involves three dimensions (an equilateral pyramid represented by a rockery for instance). The sheet of paper reinforces the two-dimensional thinking pattern and so the solution is ruled out by this subconscious assumption. Paul Sloane comments that although making assumptions will sometimes help speed things up, it will inevitably screen us from other possibilities and options. Often we will leap to the wrong conclusion and miss the chance to make a better decision.

P Sloane *Test Your Lateral Thinking IQ* (1994) p 25

A humorous example of the problem of assumptions is illustrated in the film *The Pink Panther strikes again*. Inspector Clouseau (Peter Sellers) enters a hotel lobby where there is a dog. He asks the hotel manager if his dog bites. When the manager replies 'No', he goes to stroke the dog and it bites him. Can you think what wrong assumption Clouseau made?

Well-known **lateral thinking** problems rely on people making assumptions and so ruling out the solving of the problem. Consider the following lateral thinking problems and try to think where you may be making an assumption, The first two are taken from Paul Sloane's book. The answers are given at the end of this chapter.

- **The barber paradox**: In a town there is a law that states that all men must be clean-shaven and that no man might shave himself. The only person allowed to shave people is the licensed town barber (who is forty years old). There is only one barber. Since the barber is bound by the same law, who shaves the barber?
- **The broken bag**: A healthy woman dies because the plastic bag she was carrying broke. There were many people around her at the time but they were completely unharmed. What happened?
- **Entering a field**: A woman enters a field with a pack on her back and dies. Why?
- **Pushing a car**: A man pushes a car to a hotel and then realises he is bankrupt. What happened?

3 Reasoning

While speculation is an excellent skill as it breaks the bounds of ordinary patterns that get fixed in deep grooves in our thinking processes, nevertheless the possible answers have ultimately to be logically consistent, i.e. there are no contradictions.

Philosophy has concerned itself with reasoned **arguments**. An argument can be defined as a set of statements which are such that one of them (the conclusion) is supported or implied by the others (the premises), e.g.

All human beings are mortal.
All students are human beings.
Therefore all students are mortal.

The first two statements are the premises and the third is the conclusion. A valid argument is one where there are no mistakes in logic. Hence the above argument is a valid argument. However, beware, not all valid arguments are therefore true.

> All human beings are lazy.
> All students are human beings.
> Therefore all students are lazy.

The logic is correct but the conclusion surely can't be correct! The reason is that one of the premises is untrue. Hence, even if the logic is impeccable, it does not mean to say that the conclusion is true. To acknowledge this problem, philosophy refers to an argument where both the logic is correct and the premises are true, as a sound argument.

Philosophers also distinguish between two types of argument. The first type, as exemplified above, is called **deductive**. It is such that if you agree with the premises then you would have to agree with the conclusion. Indeed, to accept the premises and deny the conclusion would be self-contradictory.

If philosophy only considered this type of argument, then disputes between philosophers would be less numerous and fewer philosophy books would be written. However, there is another type of argument that is less persuasive but more common:

> If I work hard, I will pass AS Philosophy.
> I pass AS Philosophy.
> Therefore I worked hard.

I can imagine an instance where, though I agreed with the premises, I did not agree with the conclusion. For instance, I cheated in the exam, or the examiner made a mistake when marking my paper. In other words, there are more ways of gaining a pass in AS Philosophy than working hard (though I do not recommend trying them). To express it more formally – the conclusion does not necessarily follow from the premises. The premises provide some, but not absolute, support for the conclusion.

Indeed, to accept the premises and deny the conclusion (as we have seen) would not be self-contradictory. This type of argument is called an **inductive** argument. The problem with inductive arguments is their obvious limitation of always being open to doubt and uncertainty.

Setting out arguments in a formal way – premises and conclusion – is also important for clarity. Assessing arguments becomes much easier and a basic checklist can then be followed:

- Are the premises true?
- Is the argument valid (without logical error)?
- If inductive, how persuasive is it?

4 Alternatives

If we challenge any assumptions and use reasoning, why then haven't philosophers provided us with answers to all the ultimate questions? As we noted earlier, philosophy tends to produce even more answers rather than give one single one. The fascination is that it opens up new ideas and new possibilities – things never considered before.

What this approach to thinking provides is a framework and tools to help us make up our own minds. Or to remain agnostic, but eliminating those answers that are logically inconsistent. It should help you understand why you hold a particular view. You should then be able to give reasons to justify your view and be aware of the weaknesses of alternative views, whilst, at the same time acknowledging that perhaps your own view has weaknesses as well. In this sense we talk more of probabilities than proof and possibilities rather than certainties.

Answering questions on chapter I

By the end of this chapter you should be aware of making assumptions and the need to identify and challenge any such assumptions. Also you should understand the difference between a deductive and an inductive argument.

Deductive	Inductive
If its premises are true, then its conclusion must be true	If its premises are true, then its conclusion could still be false
The premises provide absolute support for the conclusion	The premises provide some, but not absolute, support for the conclusion
The information contained in the conclusion is completely contained in the premises	

An argument is either deductive or inductive. If the premises provide no support for the conclusion then it is a non-argument.

Degree of premises' support for conclusion		
Non-arguments	**Inductive arguments**	**Deductive arguments**
None	Weak Reasonable Strong	Absolute

Solutions to the lateral thinking problems:

- Did you question the gender of the barber or assume it was a man?
- Did you assume that carrying a bag meant that it was carried by hand, carried external to the person? What about carrying something internally? True, she was healthy, but maybe she was passing through customs at an airport?
- Did you assume that the only way to enter the field was at ground level? True, maybe the pack was a pack of wolves, but it could also have been a parachute pack that was faulty.
- Did you assume the car was real? Indeed, did you assume the hotel was real? I wonder who won the game? Certainly not the person with the car!

2 Knowledge

KEYWORDS

anti-realism – truth is relative to the community who are making the statement

counter-example – a single case that shows that the claim is false

empiricism – the view that the dominant foundation of knowledge is experience

knowledge – justified true belief

necessary condition – a condition that if absent would mean that the event could not take place

objective – external to the mind, actually existing

rationalism – the view that the dominant foundation of knowledge is reason

realism – truth corresponds to the actual state of affairs

sufficient condition – a condition that if present would mean that the event is certain to take place

subjective – having its source within the mind

KEY ISSUE What are the conditions for a proposition to be classed as 'knowledge'?

1 What is real?

Recently there was a robbery reported in the paper in which the robbers had toy guns, but the guns looked so real that, just by looking you couldn't tell the difference. What looked real was in fact just an imitation, a toy. We can often be fooled by our senses. When we travel along a road on a hot day, the illusion of water on the road occurs. If you have experienced this, you will know how convincing it looks. Can you think of any more everyday illusions we experience?

These illusions raise the possibility that if we can be fooled some of the time, could it be that we are being fooled all of the time? Indeed, how can we know what is real or which things really exist?

As I said in the last chapter, the caricature of a philosopher is of someone who questions whether the table in the room really exists.

This wider doubt is actually a very disturbing question. However, it is also a kind of questioning that has become more acceptable with the popularity of science fiction and films like *The Matrix*. This film raises the possibility that none of the things we perceive at this moment are in fact real. They could all be an illusion. Maybe we are just brains in a jar, such that our bodies are illusions and we are given experiences by means of some neural manipulation. This is what is happening to the characters in *The Matrix*.

Morpheus and Neo in 'The Construct'

Neo: This isn't real...

Morpheus: What is 'real'? How do you define 'real'? If you're talking about what you can feel, what you can smell, what you can taste and see, then 'real' is simply electrical signals interpreted by your brain... (*turns on TV*) This is the world that you know. The world as it was at the end of the twentieth century. It exists now only as part of a neural interactive simulation that we call 'The Matrix'. You've been living in a dream world, Neo. (*TV switches to desolate world*) This is the world as it exists today...

Such an idea is not new. Descartes (1596–1650) suggested similar ideas in his *Meditations*, published in 1641. He attempted to examine all beliefs to see if there was a foundation of certainty – something that could not be doubted and could form the foundation for all knowledge. We will examine in detail his argument in the next chapter, but it is worthwhile tracing the development of this search for certainty and getting a broad picture of how philosophy, at various times in history, has approached this problem.

2 Epistemology

a) Meaning of epistemology

The term epistemology is used to describe a particular branch of philosophy, the branch that addresses philosophical problems concerning the theory of **knowledge**. It covers questions such as: What is knowledge and how can it be obtained?

The word epistemology is derived from the Greek words *episteme* (meaning knowledge) and *logos* (meaning study of, discourse about). The word itself is relatively new. Some would date it to the mid-nineteenth century where it began to be used to describe this area of study.

b) Brief history of epistemology

If you are new to this subject you may prefer to leave this section until you have read Chapters 3 and 4.

The discussion about how we know things and whether certainty is ever possible, is a debate that has a long history. As far back as the fifth century BCE the Greek Sophists were questioning the possibility of objective and reliable knowledge since it became clear that philosophers could not agree about the basic elements of matter and the nature and attributes of reality. The Sophists argued that human beings could only know their own perception of things, rather than the things themselves. One of the Sophists was Protagoras. (He is particularly to be commended as he is thought to be the first to teach for payment and received large sums from his students.) These Sophists were mostly sceptics who thought that there was no objective reality, and even if there were, the human mind could not fathom it (see page 37). For them what mattered was power and persuasion rather than truth.

The view propounded by the Sophists was challenged by Socrates, Plato and Aristotle. Socrates and his student, Plato, argued that certain knowledge is possible. This knowledge was about the world of unchanging and invisible ideas, and they thought that the things we experience through the senses are imperfect copies of these pure unchanging forms. Philosophy and mathematics were considered reliable vehicles to transport us to true knowledge. Aristotle emphasised experience filtered through logic as the way to gain this abstract knowledge.

After several centuries of apparent disinterest in the theory of knowledge, Thomas Aquinas (1225–1274) reawakened interest in the topic stressing reason and experience – combining logic and faith, particularly faith in the Bible – as the methods of arriving at reliable knowledge. This Aristotelian and Thomistic approach held sway until the seventeenth century.

With the Renaissance and Reformation, traditional authorities were challenged, and opponents to those authorities adopted strands of earlier Greek sceptical thought raising doubt about religious claims. If authorities like Aristotle, the Bible and the Pope could not be relied on, people began to wonder if anything was certain. It was against this background that Descartes (1596–1650) used arguments based on doubt to show that true knowledge could be discovered.

The debate between **rationalism** and **empiricism** came to the forefront during this period. Descartes argued for deductive reasoning, based on self-evident ideas, as the main source of knowledge. This view was challenged by other philosophers, particularly John Locke (1632–1704) and David Hume (1711–1776). These argued that experience was the main source of knowledge.

Immanuel Kant (1724–1804) proposed a solution that combined both rationalism and empiricism. He accepted that exact and certain knowledge was possible but this type of knowledge tells us little about the outside world, as it concerns itself more with the structure of thought. We can know things-as-they-appear (phenomena), but not things-in-themselves (noumena).

The early twentieth century saw a more pragmatic approach influenced by such movements as logical positivism. Knowledge became seen as models that attempt to represent the environment. The criterion was based on their success in problem-solving. The question of the nature of the ultimate reality behind the model was regarded as a meaningless question. Another approach has been offered by constructivism. This assumes that knowledge is constructed by the individual, without reference necessarily to objective data or innate ideas/categories. This is an **anti-realist** position about knowledge, since it opposes the **realist** theory that there are facts of knowledge independent of our knowing them. Clearly such an approach can lead to relativism where each model is regarded as being as good as any other model.

More recently the focus has been on attempting to escape this realism/anti-realism philosophical black hole. This has led to looking at our use of knowledge rather than our theories about it. One philosopher particularly associated with this approach is Edward Craig (see page 14). Another recent development has been feminist epistemology. This examines how male experiences and values have influenced the way theories of knowledge have been constructed.

3 Knowledge

a) Knowledge and its conditions

So far much mention has been made of the word knowledge. However, its exact definition has itself been an area of debate in philosophy.

Consider the following statements. Which would you consider to be knowledge?

a   The capital of Italy is Scunthorpe.
b   Brighton and Hove Albion will win the FA Cup in 2010.
c   God exists.
d   You existed yesterday.
e   The earth is the centre of the universe.

Possibly you rejected the first statement as knowledge immediately. If so, why? I expect it would have been because you know that Rome is the capital of Italy and the statement is therefore factually wrong. This implies that one condition for a statement to be classified as knowledge is that the statement must be true. Although this is one condition that is required, it clearly isn't the only one. For instance statement *b* may be true but few would want to classify that as knowledge. Does this point to another condition required for knowledge? Some people say that they know God exists, whilst others disagree. Can you identify another condition for knowledge that is required that this points to? Do you think statement *d* is knowledge? How would you convince someone that statement *d* should be classified as knowledge? Why might someone disagree?

Philosophers tend to define terms by identifying conditions. They refer to **necessary** and **sufficient** conditions. A good explanation of necessary and sufficient conditions can be found on p 5–10 in *Introduction to Philosophy* by W J Earle (1992).

In brief, a necessary condition is a property that something must have to be classified under a certain definition. If that condition is absent, then the word cannot be classified under that definition. However, that condition alone may not be enough. It is a necessary condition that oxygen must be present for fire but that condition alone is not enough to produce fire. In the discussion above we saw that just because a statement was true, we wouldn't call it knowledge, but truth was a necessary condition, for if the statement were false then we equally wouldn't use the term knowledge.

In contrast, for a sufficient condition, it would mean that it automatically warrants that definition. Being a dog is sufficient condition for being a canine.

When this approach is applied to the term knowledge, three conditions have traditionally been identified. A J Ayer (*The Problem of Knowledge*, 1974) gave the necessary and sufficient conditions for someone's (S) knowing a given proposition (P) as:

1   P is true
2   S is sure that P is true
3   S has the right to be sure that P is true.

Sometimes these conditions have been slightly rephrased with 'has the right to be sure' being substituted by 'has adequate evidence of' or 'is justified in believing'.

The definition of knowledge is usually summarised as 'justified true belief', since it has three main components:

1 An **objective** component (true)
The statement must be true. This is one way that knowledge is distinguished from 'belief', since belief can be in error. Knowledge implies 'being right' since it seems contradictory to say that you know something when that something is not actually the case. This means that something that is commonly regarded as true and called knowledge may later be found to be false and so was wrongly defined as knowledge. For instance, did you argue that statement *e* above was knowledge? It certainly would have been regarded as such before the time of Copernicus.

2 A **subjective** component (belief)
The person must believe the statement for it to be described as knowledge. Dancy (*Introduction to Contemporary Epistemology*, 1985) notes that certainty rather than belief seems to be required, though he admits that it is hard to explain why it seems a necessary condition. He suggests (p 24) that 'the notion of certainty is relevant to the analysis of claims to knowledge but not to the analysis of knowledge itself'.

In Ayer's definition used above, he has strengthened the idea of belief with the use of the phrase 'is sure that'.

Plato makes a distinction between belief and knowledge in his dialogue *Theaetetus*. He refers to a jury who, though they may believe that a defendant is guilty, cannot claim knowledge of this as they have insufficient evidence. Here he emphasises the need for some sort of justification or rationale. Hence the third condition.

3 Has a right to be sure (justified)
It is this condition that has been the most problematic. A number of counterexamples have been used to highlight the weaknesses of this condition. A counterexample is an example that shows that a certain claim is false. Hence examples have been proposed that fulfil the condition yet do not seem to be an example of knowledge.

b) Counterexamples

Hamlyn (*The Theory of Knowledge*, 1970) cites the example of 'The Rocking-horse Winner' – a D H Lawrence story in which a boy gets the winner of a horse right simply by riding a rocking-horse. Every time he rocks on it frantically in the evening, he is able to predict which horse will win a race the following day. The predictions are always right. However, would it be correct to say that the boy knew the winner? Check the conditions and see if they fit:

● The boy was correct
● The boy was sure
● The justification is that (in the story) he always got it right, therefore ruling out a lucky guess.

Many philosophers would be reluctant to call this knowledge. Does always being right count as a justification?

Consider another example. A person is certain that there is a vase on the table. She can see it. In fact she is looking at a hologram of a vase, but behind that (and unseen by the woman) is a real vase. In what sense does the woman have knowledge that there is a vase on the table? Again, you need to check the conditions given for the definition.

Perhaps the person who best drew attention to this problem of the definition is Edmund Gettier. In 1963 he wrote an article (*Analysis 23*) suggesting that having the right to believe or being justified in believing, is not in itself sufficient. It does not seem to cover the case of a justification that is irrelevant to the truth of the proposition P (i.e. the woman seeing the hologram and so justified in thinking there was a vase on the table). Gettier's own **counterexample** involved Smith and Jones applying for the same job. The president of the company assures Smith that Jones would be selected. Smith also knows a fact about Jones – namely, that Jones has ten coins in his pocket. Because Smith believes Jones will get the job, Smith is justified in believing that the man who will get the job has ten coins in his pocket i.e. Jones. In fact Smith himself gets the job and, unknown to him, he himself has ten coins in his pocket.

Now the philosophical problem is deciding whether Smith knew that the person who will get the job has ten coins in his pocket. Again, you need to check the three conditions to see if they are met. According to Gettier they are and so, either we have to count this as knowledge, or we have to add another condition.

c) Additional conditions

The debate is ongoing and can be followed in detail in *Knowledge*, edited by Sven Bernecker and Fred Dretske (2000). Likewise Dancy (*Introduction to Contemporary Epistemology*, 1985) has listed a number of ways forward (chapters 2–3) and in particular highlights the solution proposed by Robert Nozick. His solution is called the conditional theory of knowledge and attempts to remove this problem of someone's justification that is based on a reliable method, acquiring a belief that is true, but where the use of the method plays no relevant part in the success.

Nozick accepts the original first two conditions.

1   P is true
2   S is sure that P is true

He then adds two new ones that expand justification.

3   If P were not true, then S would not believe P
4   If, in changed circumstances, P were still true, S would still believe P.

For instance if you applied this to the case of the hologram vase, then using condition 3: If the real vase were not true then S would still believe P since the reason for believing is the hologram. Nozick refers to this condition as 'tracking the truth'.

Another solution has been suggested by Goldman (*Journal of Philosophy 64*, 1967). His additional condition involves causal connections. He argues that the proposition P should cause S's belief that P is true. This removes the cases where it is just coincidence that the belief happens also to be true. Again, you need to apply this to the counterexamples to see if they are eliminated.

d) Recent approaches

Craig (*Knowledge and the State of Nature*, 1990) distinguishes between our use of knowledge and our theories about knowledge. He argues that the idea of what the concept 'knowledge' actually means seems to demand more than justified true beliefs. Craig suggests that we should begin our analysis of the concept of knowledge with the purpose or meaning of knowledge rather than concern with the necessary and sufficient conditions for us to have knowledge. True beliefs are more akin to successful actions and the concept of knowledge helps flag approved sources of information.

e) Internalism and externalism

Recent epistemology has introduced the terms internalism and externalism. An internalist account of the criteria for justification requires that whatever it is that does the justification, it must be accessible to, and known to, the person. In other words, the criteria for justification depends on factors within that person's mind. In contrast, externalist accounts of the criteria for justification depend on factors outside the person. The additional conditions discussed above in c) are externalist in that they require a causal link, independent of the person expressing the belief.

f) 'Knowing that' and 'knowing how'

It should be remembered that this definition of knowledge only addresses 'knowing that'. Knowledge in the 'knowing that' sense is called propositional knowledge, since it comprises assenting to certain propositions. There is another type of knowledge called 'knowing how'. For example, I know how to drive a car. This is about ability rather than a proposition.

However, the attempt to define 'knowledge that' does raise a whole number of other issues, which in many respects overlap each other. These issues are covered in other chapters.

What constitutes justification? (chapter 6)

What are the criteria for truth? (chapter 7)

Summary diagram

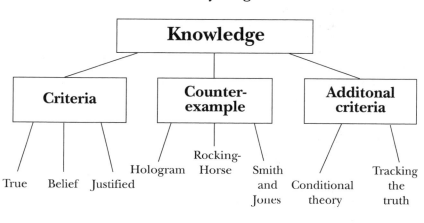

Did you manage to think of any more everyday illusions? What about the parallel railway tracks that seem to meet in the distance as we look down the straight stretch of railway line? Think also of what a stick looks like when half of it is in water.

A typical exam question on this area might ask you to 'Assess the view that justified true belief is an adequate definition for knowledge'.

This requires a candidate to understand what is involved in responding to the trigger word 'assess'. There are three assessment objectives at AS level in Philosophy. They are knowledge and understanding (AO1), selection and application (AO2) and interpretation and evaluation (AO3). When the trigger words 'assess' or 'evaluate' or 'critically examine' appear in a question, then all three assessment objectives will be examined. Hence good answers will evaluate the material they select and apply to the debate and subject arguments to critical scrutiny.

In relation to the question above a candidate would first need to explain and illustrate how knowledge has traditionally been defined by the tripartite conditions. Then the weaknesses of the justification aspect would need to be illustrated by suitable counterexamples (e.g. hologram of vase, Gettier example). The additional conditions would then be discussed and assessed. Finally, in the light of that discussion, the candidate would need to argue whether 'justified true belief' is an adequate definition for knowledge.

One of the important things to remember when critically assessing, is to develop a sustained argument that moves away from just giving a list of criticisms. Two or three criticisms discussed in depth, including some response to those criticisms, is far better than just listing ten criticisms. It is also important to explain how those criticisms reveal a weakness in the argument. Many candidates tend to leave the examiner to work out why the points listed are in fact criticisms.

3 Rationalism

KEY ISSUE What is meant by rationalism and how valid is it as a philosophical position?

1 Rationalism

At the start of the last chapter we saw that philosophers have asked some very unsettling questions about what, if indeed anything, we can know. Such questions force us to consider the foundations of our belief.

Consider one of Zeno's **paradoxes** (c.450 BCE) which implies that motion is impossible. Zeno pointed out that in order to cover any distance (let's say A to B) it is necessary first to cover half the distance, then half the remainder, then half of that remainder, and so on without limit. By that argument there would be an infinite number of distances to travel before you arrived at B. In fact you would never arrive at B. It seems that our reason is telling us one thing (motion from A to B is impossible) whilst our experience tells us another (that we do travel from A to B).

The debate about the foundation of human knowledge has gone on throughout the centuries (see page 9). However, it was during the seventeenth and eighteenth centuries that it centred on rationalism and empiricism. Rationalism is the view that we can get certainty about the world by using logic and reasoning. The term 'rationalist' derives from the Latin, *ratio*, meaning reason. Knowledge that we can have in advance of any experience is referred to as **a priori** knowledge. The three main philosophers associated with rationalism during this period are Descartes, Spinoza and Leibniz.

Rationalism is in contrast to empiricism (from the Greek *empeiria,* meaning experience) which argues that we can get knowledge of the world from our experiences. The three main philosophers associated with empiricism are Locke, Berkeley and Hume. Knowledge that can only be gained from our experiences is called **a posteriori** knowledge.

Consider how you know the following:

a   A triangle has three sides.

b   The Houses of Parliament are in London.

c   Something cannot be both true and false at the same time.

d   2 + 3 = 5

e   The railway station with the longest name in Britain is in Wales.

Which of the statements listed above do you think could be classed as *a priori* knowledge? Which of the statements listed above do you think could be classed as *a posteriori* knowledge?

It is probable that you found examples of both *a priori* and *a posteriori.* So does that mean that rationalists deny experience? Not at all. Clearly we use both experience and reason, but the rationalist is arguing that reason is the foundation of knowledge and plays the dominant role in our attempt to gain knowledge. Reason is a distinct faculty of knowledge and experience is secondary. Reason involves employing self-evident truths as well as deducing additional conclusions from them.

As early as Plato (428-347 BCE) the view was propounded that *a priori* knowledge was possible. Plato tried to show that mathematical knowledge is **innate** and not derived from sense experience. In the dialogue *Meno,* Socrates talks to a slave-boy who had no mathematical training. Through a series of questions he evokes from him Pythagoras' theorem. Plato argued that this showed that the boy had the information though it had never come into his consciousness.

This debate about innate ideas (ideas present in the mind before experience) and *a priori* knowledge came to the forefront during the seventeenth and eighteenth centuries. In philosophical history it is depicted as a hostile battle between the two philosophical groups of rationalists and empiricists. However, John Cottingham comments that these labels of rationalism and empiricism are misleading and an oversimplification since they were not two wholly distinct structures but rather

> a complex pattern of constantly overlapping and criss-crossing influences and counter-influences.
>
> J Cottingham *The Rationalists* (1988) p 2

Likewise Woolhouse makes a similar point when he states that

> the systematic use of the labels 'empiricist' and 'rationalist' is a product of nineteenth-century histories of philosophy.
>
> R S Woolhouse *The Empiricists* (1988) p2

Although this debate about the source of knowledge has a long history (see page 9) and did not start with Descartes, Descartes is a good place to start!

2 Descartes

Descartes in his study.

When Descartes (1596–1650) was a boy he was taught Aristotelian ideas such as the notion that causes were to be explained in terms of purpose, and that behaviour was in keeping with some underlying nature. This was in contrast to the new mathematics and science, which focussed on quantifying and giving explanations that were general and simple (size/shape/position/number). The new science was concerned with measurement and instruments. Descartes also lived in a time when the old authorities of Aristotle and the Church were being challenged.

In 1619, whilst sitting in a room heated only by a small stove, he meditated on the disunity and uncertainty of his knowledge compared with the certainties of mathematics. He sought to find a basis to show that all knowledge might have certainty and unity and in a blinding flash he saw the method that could achieve it. However, it was not until 1641 that he published this theory in detail in his *Meditations on First Philosophy*.

3 Descartes' arguments

Descartes is referred to as the founder of modern philosophy. He changed philosophical thinking by rejecting the usual approach of building on previous teaching, like that of Aristotle. For Descartes, certainty was based on doubt. What was required was to clear our minds of all previous beliefs and then accept only those which could not be doubted. The exercise was one of suspension of belief rather than disbelief. In order to see if there is some belief that cannot be doubted, we should temporarily pretend that everything that could be doubted is doubted. Descartes himself did not seriously doubt all things but rather devised this approach as a methodology which would reveal any certainties. On the basis of any certainty uncovered, Descartes could secure knowledge on a firm foundation. He referred to this sure foundation as the Archimedian Point (*Meditation 2*).

Georges Dicker comments

> Archimedes boasted that if he had a long enough lever mounted on one absolutely fixed and immovable point, he would be able to move the entire earth. Likewise Descartes hoped to find one absolutely certain piece of knowledge, so as to build an entire system of knowledge upon it.
>
> G Dicker *Descartes* (1993) p 43

a) The stages of doubt (*Meditations 1–2*)

● **Senses are main source of beliefs**
Descartes acknowledged that the beliefs that we accept as most certain and obvious are those based on our senses. We regard the information we get about our physical surroundings as trustworthy.

● **Senses can deceive**
However, we are also aware that at times our senses mislead us. Optical illusions are a common experience. In Meditation 6 Descartes gives the illustration of a tower that appears round from a distance but square when close up.

● **Dreams**
Descartes acknowledges that senses may be unreliable when conditions are poor or if someone is suffering madness, but that doesn't mean that they are therefore never reliable. We surely can't doubt, for example, the experience of holding a piece of paper. Nevertheless dreams are very vivid and sometimes it is impossible to distinguish between dreaming and waking experiences. However, dreams are still based on reality and mathematics is true whether awake or dreaming. There are universal notions gained from perception which are the raw materials of dreams.

● **Evil demon**

Descartes then introduces the idea of a deceiving God. He argues that it can't be said that such an omnipotent being couldn't exist otherwise, if God was not omnipotent, we are created by a being who could make errors and is limited and so we are likely to make errors. Equally we can't say that such an omnipotent being wouldn't deceive us since we know we are deceived by our senses. Towards the end of Meditation 1 Descartes comments 'I will suppose ... that some malignant demon, who is at once exceedingly potent and deceitful, has employed all his artifice to deceive me'. Hence the introduction of the evil demon means that doubt is cast on everything including the existence of the material world and mathematics. Remember that Descartes is not arguing that there is such an evil demon, merely that it is a methodological device that will sift out uncertainties.

b) The cogito argument

Given the possibility of the evil demon deceiving us, it is possible for Descartes to doubt the existence of his own body. Indeed, he questions then whether he actually exists at all. It is at this point, in *Meditation 2*, that he derives the famous **cogito** statement – 'Cogito ergo sum' (I think therefore I am). In fact the cogito statement is in another of his writings (*Discourse on the Method*, 1637) and in the Meditations he uses the phrase 'I am, I exist'. However, the term 'the cogito' is commonly used by commentators to refer to this general argument.

Descartes argues that even if he is deceived, he must exist, since to be the object of some act demands he exists. Thus Decartes has arrived, through reasoning, to something that cannot be doubted, namely, that when he is doubting he can be sure that he exists. He could not doubt that the thoughts he experienced in some way belonged to a thing which he calls 'I' or 'me'. Maybe the evil demon was producing those sensations or beliefs but that awareness of those sensations or beliefs meant that there was an awareness of the 'I' in a particular state.

So Descartes thought he had obtained knowledge that was a certainty. This truth of the existence of the 'I' could not be doubted regardless of circumstances. It was an absolute certainty. It was what philosophers call 'a necessary truth', in that it cannot not be true. It is a statement that cannot be refuted by any possible experience of the world. For rationalists, reason was a truth-finding faculty. However, whether Descartes had identified a necessary truth is questionable.

Another rationalist was Gottfried Leibniz (1646–1716). Like Descartes before him, he defended innate ideas but claimed that they were not fully formed from birth. Instead he said that experience shaped them but the raw ideas were there at the start. The mind contained potentialities which experience shaped into actualities.

c) Criticisms of the cogito argument

There have been a number of challenges to Descartes' claim that he had found a point of certainty:

i Descartes' method

- How can Descartes know that senses are wrong? This would require him to know when they are correct! However, Descartes never uses the premise that we are sometimes deceived by senses to show that his senses may always be deceptive. If he had done so, then the argument would have been invalid (for to conclude that he is always deceived makes it impossible for the premise to be true).
- He did not doubt enough. He agreed that mathematics could be in error because of the evil demon. Hence logic itself could be wrong. Yet Descartes used logic and regarded it as certain in order to reason his argument. But if logic has a possibility of being in error, then so does Descartes' argument.
- Descartes' mental activities (thought) must remain private to himself until he has proved the existence of other minds. Yet he uses language that implies existence of other minds and a common world. He is not therefore being sceptically consistent.
- Why make the cogito the Archimedian point? Surely the proof of a supremely perfect being (the ontological argument in *Meditation 5*), makes the cogito redundant.
- Doubts need grounds. The bare imaginability that P is not true is not grounds for doubting P.
- A complete deception is not a deception since there is nothing to compare it with (something fake requires the existence of something genuine).

ii The dream argument

- Dreams can be distinguished from waking experiences. Some people claim that when they are dreaming they are aware they are dreaming. Also dreams do not tend to be coherent or follow physical laws, unlike our waking world.
- It is not possible to make judgements whilst dreaming so that if anyone judged they were dreaming the judgement would be false.
- According to Descartes, you could not know you are dreaming. However, in order to know something is wrong requires you to know when something is correct. But how can Descartes know what is correct? A possible response is to say that all he is doing is casting doubt and so it is certainly valid to doubt – whether or not you can tell when it is correct.

iii The 'I'

- Many feel 'I am' is not an acceptable premise. For instance Bertrand Russell argued that it should read 'there are thoughts'. The word 'I' does

not describe a datum.
- The word 'I' when used by a speaker refers to more than just the person others see – rather it is something distinct and discernible by an inward gaze. Descartes uses 'I' in this second sense and therefore assumes something that is doubtful. In response, it is argued that Descartes regarded 'thought' as an **attribute** and not a **substance**. Every attribute must belong to a substance. Hence he concludes the existence of a substance of which the 'thought' that he perceives is an attribute, i.e. the 'I' does refer to a substance.
- Of course it could be challenged that every attribute must belong to a substance.
- Does the 'I' exist when the 'I' is not thinking?
- Some accused Descartes of a circular argument. The statement 'I doubt' already presupposes the existence of the 'I'. But surely that is what the conclusion is trying to show. It is a wrong argument to assume the truth of the conclusion in one or more of the premises.

iv The idea of 'thoughts'
- Bertrand Russell argued that Descartes' conclusions should be 'there are thoughts'. It did not follow that the something that was thinking your thoughts was you! Indeed it may be possible to have thoughts without owners. What had also not been proven was that the 'I' was a stable remaining item. For instance, do you exist when you are not thinking?
- Perhaps 'thoughts' are echoes of other people's thoughts. Therefore the conclusion is not 'I exist' but there are collective thoughts.
- What we consider 'thoughts' may actually be information passing through us. We are not the origin of the thought. Therefore it is not true to say 'I think'.
- How do we know we have a thought?
- How do you know that your belief that you have a certain thought is true?

4 Weaknesses of rationalism

Most philosophers now regard Descartes' cogito argument as a failure. As noted above, a number of criticisms could be raised against it.

Another weakness of rationalism is that from that certainty (if indeed there is such certainty) of 'I doubt therefore I exist', it is impossible to spread out to other knowledge because of the possibility of the evil demon. Descartes sought to overcome this by arguing for the existence of God, a being who possesses all attributes in perfection. God is perfect and would not deceive so we can trust that there is an external world. However, most agree that the argument for God's existence (known as the ontological argument) fails (see page 67).

As a result of this failure to find certainty, there has developed a more modest form of rationalism in which we ask which beliefs are more certain and which are less certain i.e. degrees of certainty.

5 The limits of rationalism

Certainly it does seem that Descartes' argument fails and therefore no *a priori* statement can be ascertained. However, what happens if we settled for less than certainty? Rationalism can give us reasons for our beliefs. It can weigh up beliefs and ask which ones are more certain and which are less certain. This issue of degrees of certainty will be looked at in chapter 6.

Summary diagram of Descartes' arguments

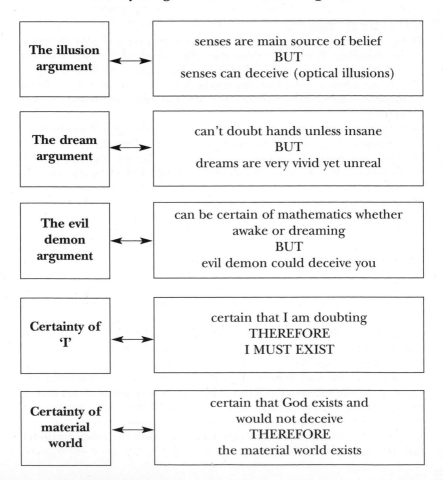

Hence a certainty has been arrived at and on the basis of this all knowledge can be built. From this certainty Descartes went on to prove that God existed and that as he was a perfect God (including perfectly good) he would not deceive us about the existence of the material world. Hence we can be sure there is a material world existing.

Answering questions on chapter 3

By the end of this chapter you should understand the terms *a priori*, *a posteriori*, rationalism and empiricism. In addition, you should be aware of the arguments for and against rationalism, and the contents and criticisms of Descartes' *Meditations 1–2*.

You might be interested in finding out about the other paradoxes of Zeno. How did you resolve the one described at the start of this chapter (page 17)? Perhaps you should consider whether it is true that the sum of an infinite collection of parts, each of which has size, must itself be an infinite size? The story of Achilles and the tortoise is a variant on the Zeno paradox, since it suggests that the tortoise is never overtaken. Remember the tortoise has a 10 metre start but runs ten times slower than Achilles. However, the tortoise has always moved on by the time Achilles gets to where the tortoise was before it moved on. Hence Achilles never overtakes the tortoise. There is a very good section on paradoxes in Roger Scruton's book *Modern Philosophy* (Sinclair-Stevenson, 1994).

Did statement *d* in the list (page 18) of *a priori/a posteriori* statements pose a problem? Philosophers disagree which category it fits into. We will consider this example in the next chapter. Can you think of arguments for regarding it as *a priori*? Can you think of arguments for regarding it as *a posteriori*?

A typical question on this topic would be 'Explain and illustrate the meaning of *a priori* and *a posteriori* knowledge'.

Explain and illustrate are non-evaluative tasks. Candidates are being asked to make clear the meaning of a particular word and to give an example. The candidate needs to point out how the example selected illustrates the term. Often candidates launch into an evaluation such as the problems of *a priori* knowledge. It should be remembered that no marks could be awarded for this since the question did not ask for that discussion. It is thus unnecessary and a poor use of time.

An evaluative question on this topic could involve assessing the success of rationalism as the basis for knowledge. Again, a sustained argument is to be preferred to a list of criticisms. The conclusion needs to have been justified in the rest of the answer.

The subject matter in this chapter also covers part of the Descartes set text. Again, set text questions cover the same three assessment objectives AO1, AO2 and AO3 (see page 15). It is important to have a thorough knowledge of the content of the set text. In AS part (a) questions on the set text, candidates are assessed on their ability to understand a given passage and it may be necessary to draw on different parts of the extract in order to provide a full response. The understanding of the passage as a whole is thereby assessed. Once again it should be noted that no evaluation is required.

Likewise, part (b) questions on the set text do not require evaluation but centre on the skills of selection and application. It is the part (c) question that is evaluative and requires a critical discussion.

4 Empiricism

KEY ISSUE What is meant by empiricism and how valid is it as a philosophical position?

1 What is empiricism?

Did you know that when a billiard ball hits another billiard ball, the impact causes the stationary ball to move? Did you know that if you throw a stone into a pond, the stone will sink? You may not regard these pieces of knowledge as particularly startling, but just think how you came to know them. Indeed, can you think of anything about the world that you know that you didn't find out about through your senses?

At the beginning of the last chapter (page 18) some statements were listed that were identified as *a posteriori* (statements *b* and *e*). That is, they could only be known after experience. Philosophers such as Locke, Berkeley and Hume favoured experience rather than reason as a means of approaching knowledge, and they represent the empiricist position in philosophy.

Empiricism is the view that experience is the dominant source of knowledge. For empiricists, experience always means sensory experience, i.e. experience that depends on one or more of the five senses. To say something is empirical is to say that it is open to the five senses (smell, touch, taste, sight, hearing). Empiricism can be about our reasons for beliefs, which they claim will always depend on empirical evidence. For example, the reason we believe a stone will sink in water is because we have always seen that happen when a stone is thrown into water. Empiricism can also be about our concepts, which it claims must always be based on ideas that are found in experience. For instance, try to imagine something that has no connection or likeness to anything that you have ever seen before.

Even science fiction characters and monsters in films seem to be adaptations of other known life forms. Consider the film *The Alien* or the Troll in *Harry Potter and the Philosopher's Stone*. Empiricists also claim that reason is derived from our experiences of the world. We reason that the pen will fall to the ground if we let go of it, since that has been our regular experience in the past.

One can see why empiricism is attractive as a theory for the source of knowledge. Did you manage to find any statements about the world that were not gained from experience? Even Descartes recognised that our senses seem the source of most of our strongest beliefs (see page 20). Our senses seem to give us a direct connection between the physical world and ourselves, so it is reasonable that this is a way of discovering facts. For discussion about the problems and theories of perception see chapter 8. Also perceptual beliefs are fairly independent of other beliefs. What we see can override previous beliefs.

2 Differences between empiricism and rationalism

One of the ways to understand the differences between rationalists and empiricists is to examine the idea of necessary truths. We looked at this idea briefly in chapter three (page 21). We have also referred to *a priori* knowledge (page 17).

Rationalists argue that there is such a thing as *a priori* knowledge. Remember Descartes claimed he had identified one in the cogito argument. However, empiricists would not deny that there was *a priori* knowledge. What they do deny is the usefulness of that knowledge. They argue that such *a priori* knowledge is not about reality.

3 The empiricists' argument

In 1689 John Locke published *Essay Concerning Human Understanding*. In *Essay II* of the book, Locke answers the question 'Whence has the mind all the materials of reason and knowledge?' His response is:

> To this I answer: from experience. In that all our knowledge is founded, and from that it ultimately derives itself.
>
> J Locke *Essay II, i.2*

Locke rejected Descartes' view that some ideas are innate (with us at birth). Instead he argued that ideas or concepts are derived either

● directly from sensation or
● from reflection upon what is given in sensation, or
● from the compounding of simple ideas into complex ideas by the mind, though these ideas still originated from sensation.

In other words what experience provides is not knowledge as such but ideas and these ideas form the material basis for knowledge. The mind at birth is a *tabula rasa* (Latin for blank tablet or slate) and acquires ideas in early life by perception and reflection so that everything we know is ultimately founded on experience. Descartes had spoken of innate ideas, but Locke claimed that children do not know that 3 + 4 = 7 until they count things (i.e. have experience in adding). He stated that

> If we will attentively consider new born children we shall have little reason to think that they bring many ideas into the world with them. For besides perhaps some faint ideas of hunger, and thirst, and warmth, and some pains, which they may have felt in the womb, there is not the least appearance of any settled ideas at all in them.
>
> J Locke *Essay I, iv.2*

Remember that innate knowledge does not demand that it had to be possessed before experience. Rather it demands only that the claim to know it does not *depend* on experience for its justification or evidence.

Descartes tends to see ideas as actually present in the mind in the way that information is present in a book, whereas Locke sees the mind as a blank sheet of paper that our experiences imprint.

4 Challenges to Locke

A number of criticisms are raised against Locke's position, and in particular his claim that there are no innate ideas.

- His usage of the word 'ideas' seems to combine two distinct fields of mental phenomena – namely sense data and concepts – both of which have been questioned. For discussion about this see E J Lowe's *Locke on Human Understanding* (Routledge, 1995) pages 19–21.
- The theory of determinism and the genome project suggests some sort of programming in humans. In particular, Noam Chomsky proposed the theory of innate universal grammar (*Language and Mind*, 1972). This argues that children must have some innate basic rules for linguistic structure in order for them to learn language so rapidly. There must be some genetically programmed language structure in the language centre of the human brain.
- Fundamental laws of logic cannot be learned as they have to be used in order to learn. For instance, the law of non-contradiction states that the same thing cannot both be and not be. This law would have to be grasped before any proposition could be regarded as true, since in regarding it as true you believe it is not false.

Can you think of any criticisms of these criticisms? Remember that the assess/evaluate element in AS requires a sustained argument and discussion rather than just a list of criticisms.

5 Hume's empiricism

Hume followed Locke but made some changes in the terminology and emphasis. He changed the term 'ideas' into 'perceptions' and divided perceptions into 'impressions' and 'ideas' (*An Enquiry Concerning Human Understanding*, 1748). Impressions are our sensations and emotions, and they impress themselves on our minds; ideas are the faint images of those in thought, reflection and imagination. This is really the difference between feeling and thinking. Hence we can see colour yet also feel fear by reflection. Equally we can have thoughts of a colour and also reflect on fear and so have thoughts of fear.

We acquire beliefs about things we are not currently experiencing because of habit. Hume rejected reason as the basis. He felt that what went under the label of reasoning was really an association of ideas (habit). Beliefs are inductive-based, such as expecting the sun to rise tomorrow. Because it has happened in the past we assume it will happen in the future. Hence we do not reason it out we merely have the belief because of habit. Similarly with moral reasoning – Hume said that it was emotion not reasoning that made us act in a certain way.

6 The limits of empiricism

Descartes showed convincingly that given the idea of an evil demon, our sense experiences are not certainties. Hence empiricism is equally doomed to failure. In addition, empiricism is about perception. But philosophy raises questions about the act of perception. How do we perceive? What is the nature of the real external world that causes our perception? How do we know our perceptions are correct? These issues are discussed in chapters 8 and 9.

Like rationalism, empiricists have had to settle for something less than certainty. They cannot know for certain that there is an external world that causes our sensations, or that people have minds. For further discussion about scepticism see chapter 5.

7 Kant's synthesis

It should be noted that philosophers distinguish between different types of rationalists. There are concept rationalists who argue that some concepts are *a priori*, and there are propositional rationalists who regard some propositions as *a priori*. Likewise there are varieties of empiricists. For instance, scientific empiricism would accept Chomsky's innate language skills but deny that anything about the nature of the world can be *a priori*.

The debate between rationalism and empiricism took a new turn with the ideas of Immanuel Kant (1724–1804). In his book *Critique of Pure Reason* (1787), he synthesised rationalism and empiricism and made the claim that there was synthetic *a priori* knowledge. He introduced two new terms – analytic and synthetic.

a) Analytic and synthetic statements

An **analytic** statement has the property that the predicate is contained in the subject. The predicate is that which is said about the subject. An example of an analytic statement is 'A triangle has three sides.' Thus 'triangle' is the subject and 'has three sides' is the predicate. When you come to analyse and examine the concept of a triangle, it becomes clear that 'having three sides' is part of the concept. As you can see, an analytic statement does not contain any new information but clarifies the term.

Analytic statements can be true or false. The proposition 'All bachelors are married' is analytic but false. It is analytic because the married state is part of the concept of 'bachelor'. The fact that it is analytic does not tell you whether it is true or false, but merely how to decide whether it is true or false. The way to decide is by considering the meaning of the words.

A statement such as 'The cat sat on the mat' is clearly not an analytic statement, since there is nothing in the analysis of the concept of 'cat' that contains the idea of 'sitting on the mat'! Statements like these that add new information are called **synthetic**. Their truth value (i.e. whether they are true or false) is not able to be determined just by examining the meaning of the words.

If you want to test yourself to make sure you understand the terms analytic and synthetic, then check which of the following statements are synthetic.

a I have two hands.
b The circle is round.
c The box is on the table.
d The battle of Hastings was in 1066.
e The battle of Hastings was in 1166.

b) Analytic and synthetic truths

Both rationalists and empiricists agree that there are analytic truths and these are known *a priori*. Using the example above, neither would contest the truth of 'A triangle has three sides'. Nor would they disagree that it was known *a priori*. However, rationalists would also claim that you could have *a priori* knowledge of things about the world. In contrast, empiricists reject such a claim. They argue that no new forms of knowledge are possible unless they are derived from experience i.e. human reason or thought cannot, by itself, produce new knowledge. All such truths must be derived from experience (*a posteriori*).

Hence, for the empiricist, *a priori* knowledge consists of analytic truths that cannot tell you anything about the world but merely give the meaning of words. Such knowledge is trivial. The empiricist A J Ayer claimed all analytic propositions were **tautologies** and devoid of factual content (*Language, Truth and Logic*, 1971). Like the rationalists Kant was claiming that there was knowledge of the world and not just of language (analytic), that was known independent of experience (*a priori*). It also meant that such knowledge could not be refuted by any possible experience of the world.

c) The synthesis

Kant's synthesis is so named because he claimed

> knowledge came from a synthesis of experience and concepts: without the senses we should not become aware of any object, but without understanding we should form no conception of it.
>
> R Osborne *Philosophy for Beginners* (1992) p 103

The source of *a priori* knowledge is not experience, but its only subject matter is objects of possible experience. Robert Solomon comments:

> The truths are synthetic because they are not mere tautologies, not merely trivially true. They are *a priori* because, like all necessary truths, they are 'prior' to experience. What would our experience of the world be like if we didn't impose these forms on it? The answer is that we would not have anything we could really call 'experience'.
>
> R Solomon *The Big Questions* (1998) p 163

Both rationalists and empiricists had been arguing from the premise that our minds reflect the nature of reality. What Kant argued was that what we have viewed as reality reflects the nature of our minds. Hospers uses the illustration of us always wearing green glasses; we could never remove them and didn't know we had them on.

> ...everything would look green to us – not that everything would be green, but that it would appear so to us, because of the nature of the lenses through which we looked at it. It is not the world 'as it is in itself' that we perceive, but the world as it is filtered through our senses and our understanding.
>
> J Hospers *An Introduction to Philosophical Analysis* (1997) p 138

Now if we replaced the green glasses with assertions about space and time, then we would understand objects in a three-dimensional space and whatever events occur, they would take place in a single-time series. The world as it appears to us must have this spatial and temporal character, just as the world will appear green if we wear the green glasses.

The objects that we receive from our sensory experience are understood through our concepts or categories (e.g. space and time). Knowledge is therefore limited to appearances (phenomena), but things in themselves (noumena) are unknowable. That the phenomenal world will have these features of space and time is both synthetic and *a priori*. It is impossible to think of an object that does not occupy space and time.

Kant had other categories by which we always interpret the sensory experiences. These include perceiving the world in terms of:

- substance – things and their properties
- causality – cause and effect
- number – a certain number of things

The propositions that Kant regarded as synthetic and *a priori* included:

- arithmetical e.g. $7+5=12$
- geometrical e.g. a straight line is the shortest distance between two points
- scientific e.g. every event has a cause
- metaphysical e.g. the soul is a substance

An area that is much debated is whether Descartes argued for synthetic *a priori* knowledge. Of course even if he did, he would not have used those terms as they came into use after the time of Descartes. Certainly many argue that the cogito is synthetic since it is based on experience. His argument for God using the ontological form is analytic and so all truth ultimately relies on God. In one sense, for Descartes, God seems to occupy the same role as the synthetic *a priori* does for Kant.

8 Criticisms of Kant

- A priori knowledge implies necessity i.e. it cannot not be true; no possible experience could refute it. However, it is contingent (need not be, could be different without any logical contradiction) that our faculties are the way they are. As James Van Cleve comments 'might we not wake up tomorrow and find that cubes have thirteen edges?' (*A Companion to Epistemology*, 1992). Our faculties might change the way we see the world and therefore propositions that we made regarding the world would also change.

● Is 7 + 5 = 12 really synthetic *a priori* knowledge? Philosophers disagree about this. Is it not analytic in that its truth is derived from the meaning of the symbols +, =, 5, 7? In defence of Kant, Charles Landesman comments that

> the concept '12' does not include the idea of an operation; in fact, 12 is a value for an infinite number of different operations.

> C Landesman *An Introduction to Epistemology* (1997) p 169

● Modern science questions some basic beliefs about our world such as every effect has a cause.
● How can Kant state there is a noumenal world since it cannot be observed?

Summary diagrams

Philosophers' timeline

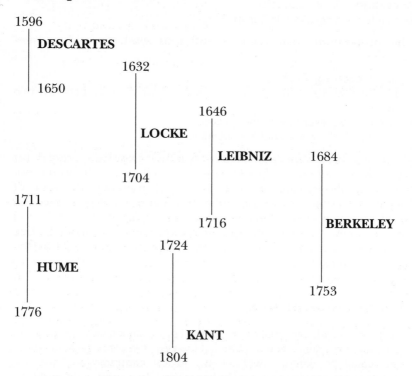

Analytic and synthetic propositions

Analytic proposition	Synthetic proposition
The square has four sides.	The cat is on the mat.
The predicate is contained in the subject.	The predicate is NOT contained in the subject.
The negation of a true analytic proposition leads to a self-contradiction.	The negation of a true synthetic proposition does not lead to a self-contradiction.
The truth value is determined by the meaning of the words.	The truth value is NOT determined by the meaning of the words.
The truth value is determined without reference to the five senses.	The truth value is usually determined by reference to the five senses.
They are mainly associated with rationalism.	They are mainly associated with empiricism.
They tell us about ideas.	They tell us about reality.
They are known *a priori*.	They are known usually *a posteriori*.

Answering questions on chapter 4

By the end of this chapter you should understand the terms analytic and synthetic. You should also know the arguments for and against empiricism and Kant's contribution to the debate.

Did you manage to challenge the criticisms listed on page 29. You may want to consider whether the Chomsky argument pays too little attention to the part imitation and practice play in the learning process. Indeed it raises the question as to how you can differentiate between innate and acquired knowledge. The law of non-contradiction would also be a problem to show that it was innate. The law states that something cannot be and not be, at the same time. However, what sort of behaviour/actions would children need to demonstrate to show that they knew this law? The law itself prevents the possibility of there being evidence, since contradictory events cannot be performed. In reply, perhaps it could be argued that children could be observed attempting such actions, and so demonstrate that they do not in fact know the law. The question now arises as to whether such actions have been observed.

Of the list of statements on page 31 only one was not synthetic and that was statement *b*. In all the others the subject was not contained in the predicate, whereas the reference to 'a circle' includes the shape of 'roundness'. Possibly statement *e* caused you to hesitate. Students often confuse analysis of type (analytic/synthetic) with truth value (whether something is true or false). Whether something is true or false makes no difference to whether something is analytic or synthetic. The term 'analytic' and 'synthetic' refer to the structure of a statement (i.e. the relationship between the subject and the predicate). *A priori* and *a posteriori*, refer to the method of knowing whether a statement is true or false.

A typical question based on this chapter might be ' Assess the view that all of our concepts are derived from experience'.

The trigger word 'assess' tells you that it is evaluative and all three assessment objectives (AO1, AO2, AO3) are expected to be demonstrated. Knowledge and understanding would involve reference to empiricists and their views about ideas being the source of our concepts and that our minds have these ideas impressed upon them by experiences. The selection and application skills would require illustrations of concepts from experience as well as some that were not from experience. Note that instincts (such as hunger, thirst or breathing) are not the same as concepts or propositional knowledge. Kant's synthesis would also be useful material to refer to since he suggests key concepts are innate and are needed to interpret the experiences. The interpretation and evaluation assessment objective would be expecting a discussion on whether all our concepts or some were derived from experience. Remember that whatever conclusion you come to it must be supported by the rest of the answer and argued for. A good answer will acknowledge different views and indicate their weaknesses.

5 Scepticism

KEYWORDS

dogmatism – an opinion/statement that is asserted as if authoritative and unchallengeable

ordinary doubt – only propositions that are genuinely doubted, are doubted

philosophical doubt – any proposition which is logically possible to doubt, is doubted

scepticism – the view that we can know very little, perhaps nothing at all

solipsism – the belief that only oneself and one's experiences exist

KEY ISSUE If we have no innate concepts and we can't trust experience, then in what sense can we know anything at all?

1 What is scepticism?

After watching a film like *The Matrix*, in which all reality is questioned, we realise we may not be sure about anything and so lack certainty. Such a view is known as scepticism. The word **scepticism** comes from the Greek *skeptikos* which literally means inquiring. Hence a sceptic was someone who had not yet reached firm beliefs but was still seeking answers and inquiring. It developed into a philosophical position holding the view that humans lack knowledge. The degree of scepticism could vary from complete (global) scepticism, in which it is claimed nothing can be known, to partial (local) scepticism, that holds that humans lack knowledge in certain areas/topics.

2 Brief history of scepticism

The history of scepticism falls into two main periods. The first is during the Hellenistic age when sceptical schools emerged in Greece. The first formulation of the ideas of scepticism into a philosophical school (Pyrrhonism) is usually attributed to Pyrrho of Elis (365–270 BCE). He argued that the reasons in favour of a belief are never better than those against it and so inquiry is unproductive. One should suspend judgement altogether so that peace of mind could be achieved. Various anecdotes about him appear in the writings of Diogenes Laertius (third century CE), including stories where he apparently needed constant protection from falling over precipices because he refused to accept the testimony of the senses.

The second main period arose in the fifteenth and sixteenth centuries. As was seen in chapter 3 with Descartes, there was intellectual ferment resulting from battles between different theological positions and from the challenge posed by the new sciences.

3 Reasons for scepticism

There is a tension between wanting to believe truth yet also wanting to avoid falsehood. The first encourages us to believe readily, whilst the latter encourages us to suspend judgements. The result is to be driven to believing only that which is conclusive and certain. However, there seems only two ways to know something. It is either from innate ideas (*a priori*) or from our senses (*a posteriori*). We have already seen in chapter 3 that it is doubtful whether any *a priori* propositions about the world have been established. The cogito seems to fail.

Equally, evidence from our senses (*a posteriori*) seems unreliable. Whilst I find it difficult to believe that I am hallucinating when I get into my car to drive to Worthing College, I acknowledge that I would find it difficult to believe I was hallucinating if I really were, provided the hallucination was vivid. Thus neither *a priori* nor *a posteriori* approaches lead to certainty. As Hilary Putman noted, we could all be a brain in a vat, stimulated electrically in such a way as to give us the delusive experience of living the life with which we are familiar (*Reason, Truth, and History,* 1981).

Another argument that supports scepticism is called 'the infinite regress problem'. If every belief that constitutes indirect knowledge is based on knowledge of something else, or a further belief, then the sequence will require further knowledge to base that belief on, and so on. In short, the sequence will regress infinitely and be unanchored. Therefore, unless there is direct knowledge somewhere in the sequence, there will be no final basis to the sequence of knowledge. As we shall see in chapter 6, infinite regression is also a problem for justification criteria.

From these arguments it seems that we do not have knowledge since there are always grounds to doubt the evidence. We are also aware that our supposed certainty is sometimes shown to be wrong. The possibility of error cannot therefore be excluded and, until we can exclude the possibility of being wrong, we are not justified in claiming certainty. This leads us to scepticism.

4 Types of doubt

a) Philosophical doubt

This is the type of doubt that would drive you insane if you consistently applied it. Indeed, Hume said that you must leave it behind in the philosophy room and ignore it in the rest of life. It demands that every proposition is subject to **philosophical doubt** if there is a logical possibility that it could be false. An example of philosophical doubt is where all empirical evidence would be doubted as would our reasoning abilities. This corresponds to global scepticism if the *a priori* and *a posteriori* are doubted. However, as we saw with Descartes in chapter 3, it is not usually genuine uncertainty but rather a methodological tool.

Try to live the next thirty minutes applying philosophical doubt. Think of some of the things you would doubt. How would it affect the way you lived your life?

b) Ordinary doubt

In contrast to philosophical doubt is **ordinary doubt**, or mitigated scepticism, as Hume referred to it. This arises from an awareness of a lack of evidence (empirical) or a distrust in one's reasoning (mathematical/logical) or from some deficiency of skill/expertise which requires specialised knowledge to judge or produce evidence. Whereas philosophical doubt was a methodological device, ordinary doubt entails genuine uncertainty which may be quite deep so that actions/conclusions cannot be decided, or a minor worry which might make actions/conclusions tentative. An example of ordinary doubt is a 'reasonable doubt in court of law'.

Can you think of some things about which you express ordinary doubt? How does this affect the way you live your life?

5 The merits of philosophical doubt

As Descartes illustrated, philosophical doubt can be positive. For instance,

- It is a tool whereby the grounds for knowledge are rigorously contested and clarified.
- It brings to light any hidden assumptions.
- It promises the establishment of a firmer basis for knowledge.
- It encourages a critical approach and prevents easy acceptance of taken for granted assumptions.
- It checks passions and prejudices.
- It challenges **dogmatism**.

● It stops the learned getting proud.
● It reminds us that facts are theory laden.
● It promotes consideration of alternative explanations and ideas.

6 Is total scepticism possible?

Thomas Nagel (*The View from Nowhere*, 1986) argued that scepticism is inescapable if one takes a realist view about our knowledge of the external world. It is impossible to eliminate subjectivity (the view from nowhere) from which all things can be known. Therefore our knowledge is necessarily limited. We can't see everything all at once.

Hume considered that total scepticism was not only difficult but also undesirable. In the closing section of the *Enquiry* he warned

> But a Pyrrhonian cannot expect that his philosophy will have any constant influence on the mind: or if it had, that its influence would be beneficial to society. On the contrary, he must acknowledge, if he will acknowledge anything, that all human life must perish, were his principles universally and steadily to prevail. All discourse, all action would immediately cease; and men remain in a total lethargy, till the necessities of nature, unsatisfied, put an end to their miserable existence.

> D Hume *Enquiry, Section XII, part II*

However Hume did not think that such global scepticism could be consistently maintained by anyone. Rather it was something that was entertained in the philosophy class but then abandoned as soon as you left the classroom.

> These principles may flourish and triumph in the schools; where it is, indeed, difficult, if not impossible, to refute them. But as soon as they leave the shade, and by the presence of the real objects, which actuate our passions and sentiments, are put in opposition to the more powerful principles of our nature, they vanish like smoke, and leave the most determined sceptic in the same condition as other mortals.

> D Hume *Enquiry, Section XII, part II*

Total scepticism can lead to a position known as **solipsism**. This is a belief that only oneself and one's experiences exist. Such a person denies the existence of the external world including other people. Simon Blackburn (*The Oxford Dictionary of Philosophy*, 1994) records the story of the philosopher Bertrand Russell meeting a woman who claimed she was a solipsist. In conversation the woman expressed surprise that more people were not solipsists!

Other reasons to oppose the position of global scepticism include:

- If we have no grounds for belief, we have no grounds for doubt.
- The total sceptic seems to leave us with the certainty that we cannot have certainty.
- Universal possibility of error does not imply that everything is error. The fact that we might be mistaken does not mean that we are.
- If nothing can be known, then how can the sceptic know they are being deceived?
- There can't be total doubt as doubt is a parasite of knowledge. To say that a coin is a fake only makes sense if there is such a thing as a real coin to which you are comparing it.
- The common sense argument contends that scepticism provides no good argument against common sense. Merely suggesting doubt is possible and not logically contradictory, is not, in itself, sufficient reason to doubt. They may be all capable of doubt by the sceptic, but they may not all be equally doubt worthy. We shall consider the issue of justification criteria in the next chapter.
- The private language argument was proposed by Ludwig Wittgenstein (1889–1951). Speaking a language is regarded as an acquired skill. A criterion of success is required to check correct application of the vocabulary. The check for language about sensations must be independent and therefore requires the notion of a public world. Language uses rules so that words keep the same meaning. If it is not checked for meaning and usage in the public world (other people) then there would be no way to tell the difference between being right and seeming to be right. Memory would not be sufficient because the memory could be in error. Hence global doubt is impossible since if language exists there must at least be other minds/people. In summary, private language is impossible and solipsism is untenable.

Summary diagram
Philosophical doubt

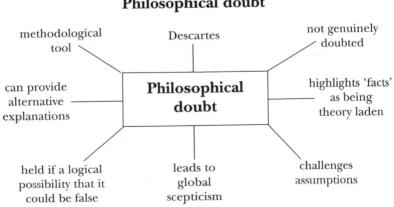

Try to do a similar diagram for ordinary doubt.

Answering questions on chapter 5

By the end of this chapter you should understand the differences between philosophical and ordinary doubt. Also you should be able to assess the arguments for and against global scepticism.

If you applied philosophical scepticism for thirty minutes, I wonder what things you included. Of course, you should include everything, since nothing can escape it! As you can imagine, this would have serious consequences on your everyday life.

A typical question on this topic is 'Briefly explain what is meant by the claim that philosophical doubt leads to solipsism'.

This is testing the knowledge and understanding assessment objective and so no evaluation is required. Candidates would be expected to show knowledge of the technical words by defining 'philosophical doubt' and 'solipsism'. They would need to show understanding by relating the consequences of philosophical doubt, such as rejection of *a priori* and *a posteriori*, showing that it leads to the state of solipsism.

Remember that the marks awarded to a question indicate how much time candidates are expected to spend answering it. If the exam is an hour and the question is worth 6 marks out of a total of 45 possible marks for the whole exam, then no more than about 8 minutes should be spent on it. Often candidates repeat illustrations that add nothing new to those already given and so waste time. If a question is worth 15 marks out of the 45, then about 20 minutes should be spent on it and most candidates would write about 300 words in that time.

6 Justification

KEYWORDS

coherentism – the view that a set of propositions may be known without a foundation in certainty but by their interlocking strength

foundationalism – justification based upon secure certain foundations that require no further justification

justification – reasonable grounds

reliabilism – justification that is based on a reliable method

KEY ISSUE Beliefs need some support, but what actually counts as support? What seems a reason to one person does not always persuade others.

1 What is justification?

In chapter 2 (page 12) knowledge was defined as justified true belief. We saw that having a true belief isn't sufficient for knowledge. A lucky guess may be a true belief but few would want to describe it as knowledge. In addition to true belief, knowledge requires us to have a reason to believe or evidence in favour or some sort of **justification** for believing. Reason, evidence and justification all have similar meanings. They express the notion that beliefs need some sort of support, such that some explanation is given for holding a particular belief. There is a difference between knowing a belief is justified and a belief being justified.

Consider the beliefs listed below that some people might hold, and suggest the justification that they might give for regarding such beliefs as true.

- *a* Capital punishment is wrong.
- *b* If I let go of this pen it will drop to the floor.
- *c* Grass is green.
- *d* Everyone had four grandparents.
- *e* There is no intelligent life on other planets of our solar system.

A number of justifications could have been listed. These could have ranged from reliance on a religious authority to reasoning from evidence from scientific method and the uniformity of nature or perhaps appeals to logic.

Can you now think how you could challenge those justifications? Do they rely on further beliefs that can also be challenged? (For further comments about these beliefs see the end of this chapter.) This search for some ultimate justification has led philosophers to develop a number of approaches or theories.

2 Theories of justification

We saw that one argument in favour of scepticism is the infinite regress of beliefs (page 38). Some beliefs are justified by being based on, or inferred from, further supporting beliefs. If every supporting belief could only be justified by yet further beliefs, there would have to be an infinite regress of justifications. No beliefs would be ultimately justified since there would be no end to them. There are four main responses to this problem.

- The regression does not stop but goes on forever. However, this is not a problem.
- The regression eventually circles back around to some of the beliefs it started with. This approach is called **coherentism**.
- The regression stops with beliefs that are justified but don't get their justification from any further beliefs. This approach is called **foundationalism**.
- The regression stops with beliefs that are not themselves justified but follow a reliable method. This approach is called **reliabilism** or probabilism.

a) Regression is not a problem

This argues that we should accept that justification continues ad infinitum. Why should it be a problem to us since we experience the concept of infinity in other areas of our thinking without trying to eliminate it, e.g. a finite line can be divided infinitely. If all justification is inferential then the definition of knowledge will have to be adapted to allow for this state of affairs. The alternative would be to deny that knowledge is possible.

b) Coherentism

The coherentist favours a form of justification that is more circular than linear. The term coherent has a particular meaning when used in this special sense referring to forms of justification. In the non-technical sense 'incoherent' has the meaning of being incomprehensible or nonsensical. However, when we state that a set of beliefs is coherent, in the technical sense, we are claiming that they are logically consistent and fit together in ways that let them explain and help support each other. For instance the set of beliefs, *Charles lives in Malta, Malta is an independent country*, is not a coherent set of beliefs because its members do not support each other. However, if we were to add a third member to this set, namely, *Charles holds a Maltese passport*, then we can make the set coherent. The fact that Charles holds a Maltese passport supports the statement that he lives in Malta and is consistent with the fact that Malta is an independent country and therefore issues its own passports. Of course it does not demonstrate certainty. Most coherentists are regarded as internalists (see page 14) since they claim that justification is a matter of internal relations between beliefs. It might well be the case that these beliefs do not correspond to external reality.

So what does coherency achieve?

Coherency can have both a negative and a positive role. It can be used in a negative sense in that it can reveal beliefs that are incoherent and so are not justified. This would mean, for example, that a set of beliefs was logically inconsistent and so they could not all be held simultaneously. In a positive role, coherentism can generate justification and is therefore sufficient to make the set of beliefs justified.

This type of justification is viewed as circular rather than linear because coherentists demand that all beliefs get their justification from their relationship to other beliefs and never from 'outside' the system of beliefs. For example, most coherentists believe that our senses are reliable. But this is derived, in turn, from other particular perception beliefs where all our senses cohere to what we experience, e.g. falling over and hurting ourselves. The many aspects of that experience all cohere to the experience happening in the way that we think it did.

The criticisms raised against such a theory of justification include:

- The problem of infinite regress. If justification of belief D involves beliefs A, B and C, then how do I justify beliefs A, or B or C? At some stage a priority of beliefs has to be established. However, the problem of infinite regress makes this impossible, since justification of a belief is only granted in terms of greater or lesser coherency in relationship to other beliefs.
- False beliefs could cohere just as much as true beliefs. Truth would be reduced to a subjectively justified view which has implications for the theory of truth (see chapter 7). For instance, if you thought that aliens were living next door to you, then it is possible that all events that happen will be seen as coherent with this view. Indeed, can you state what would have to happen for this view to be proved false?
- It assumes a very strong confidence in the ability of mental reflection to lead to truth. This is a general weakness of any internalist approach.

Some have responded to the problem of infinite regress by emphasising the holistic nature of the coherency approach to justificatión. Holism is the view that whole theories are the units of confirmation, rather than one foundational belief (see below, foundationalism). Hence, whether a belief is justified depends upon the support of the whole structure of beliefs to which it belongs. Dancy (*Introduction to Contemporary Epistemology*, 1985) suggests that perhaps coherentism escapes the infinite regress problem because of its holistic approach. For instance it could be argued that coherentism is conditional upon the presence of a set of beliefs but not the justification of that set of beliefs (pages 128–129).

c) Foundationalism

Foundationalist theories assert that there is a class of beliefs called basic beliefs, which do not require any evidence. These foundational beliefs support others which form the superstructure. There are two main schools of foundationalists – the classical and the modest.

Classical foundationalism believes that basic beliefs are self-justified. They are classed as self-justified

i) if it is impossible for a person to be mistaken about a particular belief, e.g. I am in pain

ii) if a proposition must be known to be true once it is understood, e.g. $1 + 1 = 2$.

Besides being infallible these foundational beliefs also have to be incorrigible (cannot be shown to be mistaken) and indubitable (cannot be doubted). Further beliefs (superstructure) are justified by logical connections derived from basic beliefs.

In contrast, modest foundationalists only claim about the source of their beliefs and make no pronouncements as to their infallibility. All that matters is that the beliefs do not come from other beliefs. In that sense they are foundational. Hence, some may include as foundational such things as intuition or that it feels right. Some may accept only those beliefs that are self-justified whilst others may include perceptual beliefs about the external world. Some foundationalists are rationalists whilst others could be empiricists. Modest foundationalists also allow other justifications for further beliefs besides logical connections, e.g. coherency. Most contemporary foundationalists are modest foundationalists.

The main weakness of the classical foundationalist's position is justifying the infallibility of the basic belief.

● It could be argued that even our description of our sensory state could be in error.
● No basic beliefs can be identified, e.g. cogito failure (see page 22).
● Any such basic belief will by necessity have insufficient content to support the superstructure.

d) Reliabilism

Reliabilism argues that for beliefs to be justified they must be based on a reliable process, i.e. one that produces a good rate of success. These processes could include logic or our memory. They have been regarded as reliable in the past, in the sense that we have taken them to be processes that lead to truth. We usually regard something as a reliable process if it leads to a correct prediction, description, identification or explanation. Hence, random guessing cannot justify beliefs as it is not regarded as a reliable process. Reliabilism is classified as an externalist theory because the approach is an appeal to truth that is external. Using the criteria of reliabilism, it is not possible to tell whether the beliefs are justified using only introspection and reflection. Hence the facts about the beliefs which determine whether or not they are justified are not internally available to us. Goldman argues that an additional condition is needed to eliminate the counterexample where the process as a general process is reliable but in a particular circumstance is unreliable. He suggests that all beliefs produced by reliable processes (of the sort that require no beliefs as input) are justified, unless they are undermined.

Another approach similar to reliabilism is probabilism. This sees the truth of beliefs in terms of degrees of probability. Justification occurs if the probabilities do not violate any of the axioms of the probability calculus. This probability approach changes justification to degrees of belief rather than 'all-or-nothing' belief.

Criticisms raised against reliabilism include:

- Circularity and infinite regression are not avoided. For instance, how does one know what is a reliable process? If I remember past occasions where the outcome was successful it presupposes that my memory is a reliable process. But how can that be justified?
- The requirement is that the reliable process is not undermined in some way. However, how would that ever be known? Surely the process on previous occasions may have been undermined.
- To know something is reliable requires you to already rely on it to find out that it is reliable.

Summary diagram

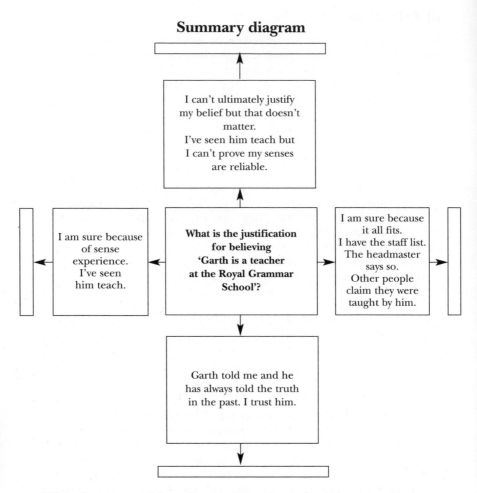

Fill in the name of the relevant theory in each of the empty boxes.

Answering questions on chapter 6

By the end of this chapter you should understand the approaches of coherentism, foundationalism and reliabilism as theories of justification. You should be able to argue the strengths and weaknesses of each approach.

The challenges to the set of beliefs listed on page 43 should have highlighted the difficulties involved in justifying a belief. Finding a starting point that does not require further justification is problematic. For instance, in example *a*, people may appeal to the belief in the sanctity of life to justify calling capital punishment wrong. However, what is the justification for the sanctity of life? If some religious authority is appealed to, then what is the justification for regarding that source as an authority?

In example *b*, the uniformity of nature may be appealed to as a justification, together with our past experiences. However, these require a belief in our memory being accurate and the belief that, because we have not seen any exceptions to the laws of nature, then there have not been any. Equally the belief is implied that what happens in the past will happen in the future. Each of these beliefs requires a further justification.

Example *c* assumes beliefs about our perception that will be considered in chapter 9. Did you regard example *d* as certain, possibly appealing to logic? If so, then you would have to justify why you believe logic will lead you to truth. In fact the belief that everyone has four grandparents is misplaced. Can you think of a case where someone never had four grandparents?

Disagreements over the truth of example *e* will reveal that we all put beliefs in a hierarchical order. When this order differs between people then we have disagreements. This suggests that investigating the justification for beliefs is essential when arguing about beliefs. It will highlight the fundamental reason for the disagreement. This is particularly important in moral arguments. An appeal for justification such as 'because the Bible says so', will hold very little sway with those who do not hold a belief that the Bible is a source of authority.

A typical exam question on this topic would be 'Identify one strength and one weakness of reliabilism as a theory of justification'.

The trigger word 'identify' is not evaluative. You would need to define reliabilism. Then it is important to, not only state the strength and the weakness, but also to explain in what way they are a strength and weakness respectively. For instance a strength might be that it uses processes that have already been successful. Some illustration of this would be helpful together with an explanation why that should be seen as a strength. For the weakness, circularity and infinite regression would be suitable to discuss. Again, an example would help together with the explanation of why it constitutes a weakness.

7 Theories of Truth

KEYWORDS

correspondence theory – this claims that a statement is true if it corresponds to something in the real world

coherency theory – this claims that a statement is true if it coheres with other statements

pragmatic theory – this claims a statement is true if it is useful and works

language-games – a term used by Wittgenstein to refer to any particular context in which language is used. It is the use of the word that gives it its meaning

picture theory of language – the meaning of a word is knowing what it pictures in the real world

KEY ISSUE Pilate is reported to have asked Jesus 'What is truth?'. Philosophers have been asking the same question down the centuries.

South East Essex College
of Arts & Technology
Luker Road, Southend-on-Sea, Essex SS1 1ND
Tel:(01702) 220400 Fax:(01702) 432320 Minicom (01702) 2...

1 Truth

In chapter 1 (page 4) a sound argument was distinguished from a valid argument. Both had no errors in logic, but the sound argument had the additional condition that the premises had to be true. Truth is something that we are concerned about. In chapter 2 we discussed what was meant by the word 'knowledge' and found that it involved the criterion of truth. In the last chapter we considered the criteria for justifying a belief, and when such criteria are met it is usually considered grounds for thinking that the belief is true. However, the issue of what exactly is meant by 'true' is the subject of this chapter.

For each of the following statements, say what is meant by the claim that the statement is true.

a   There is a table in the library of Edinburgh University.
b $2 + 3 = 5$
c   The Empire State Building is not in Clacton-on-Sea.
d   The Quantum Theory describes the behaviour of subatomic particles.
e   The boat crossed the equator line.
f   God exists.

Most people would regard statement *a* as a description of an actual state of affairs in the world, in this case in Edinburgh. However, is statement *b* describing something in the world? Indeed, in what sense do numbers actually exist as things in the world? And what of statement *c*, where the fact seems to be something that is not the case? It seems that what we mean by 'true' is more complex than at first appeared. Is it possible to see the equator line? If not, then in what sense is it a description of the world? Is God an object, an item in the universe, or is it just a word we use to express an idea that is important to us?

The exact meaning of the concept of truth has occupied philosophers through the centuries. There have developed three main philosophical theories of truth:

- the correspondence theory
- the coherency theory
- the pragmatic theory.

2 The correspondence theory

Aristotle is often quoted in respect of describing the **correspondence theory**:

> to say that (either) that which is is not or that which is not is, is a falsehood: and to say that that which is is and that which is not is not, is true.

Aristotle

However, a more modern formulation can be found in Landesman's book:

> The impulse behind this correspondence theory of truth is the idea that the truth of what we say or think depends not upon what we happen to believe, but upon the way the world is. What we think is true or false depends upon whether or not there is something in the world that answers to it. Thus ... there is a world that is independent of thought and belief that we aim to learn about in our inquiries.

C Landesman *An Introduction to Epistemology* (1997) p 132

Hence true propositions correspond with reality and are not mind-dependent. It is that correspondence that makes them 'true'. The correspondence theory favours a version of realism which claims that external things are independent of how we might perceive them to be. When we say that 'the cat sat on the mat' we are claiming that the statement is true because there is something that is in the real world that it corresponds to; namely, an animal that is a cat, and the cat's posture is that it is sitting on the mat. In this view of truth we discover reality, make statements about it, and truth emerges in terms of how well those statements correspond to reality.

Plato and Aristotle.

Wittgenstein gave some support to this approach to truth when he argued for a **picture theory of language** (*Tractatus Logico-Philosophicus*, 1922). This stressed that language had to be about something other than language. Meaningful language involved words being defined by the real world of objects. The meaning of a proposition lay in knowing what is pictured. To understand a proposition means to know what is the case if it is true.

Although this is probably the most popular view of truth held by people, it is not without its critics. For instance:

● Some statements do not have a correspondence to reality. For example, 5 + 7 = 12, or 'If the atomic bomb had not been dropped on Japan the war would have lasted another two years'. What kind of truths are these?

● It is an oversimplified view of how we determine truth. It is not possible to check each statement against reality. It is a belief that involves a complex web of other beliefs.

● Hosper (*An Introduction to Philosophical Analysis*, 1997) comments that a statement by itself corresponds to a fact only if the speaker intends it for that purpose.

● Wittgenstein later rejected his picture theory view of language in favour of **language-games** (*Philosophical Investigations*, 1953).

● Realism has to be assumed, since a real world that can be perceived is basic to the correspondence theory.
● Robert Solomon points out that

> any claim to know the truth requires that we know the facts independently of our claim to know the truth, in order to justify our claim to the truth. We need the truth (the facts) in order to justify our claim to the truth.

R Solomon The Big Questions (1998) p 169

But how can we know the world apart from our own knowledge? Perhaps there is confusion between the criteria for justifying truth and truth itself?

3 The coherency theory

As we saw above, mathematical truths do not have a corresponding reality. A similar thing can be said about moral/ethical statements. From this it can be seen that truths are not always descriptions of reality.

The coherency theory makes truth a matter of statements cohering with other statements. Not only must they be consistent with each other, but they must support one another and provide evidence for each other. Certainly this approach does reflect the way many people think of truth. Earle gives the example of a poltergeist being blamed for disarranging a study. The poltergeist explanation is rejected

> because it doesn't fit in with – or cohere with – the bulk of what (the person) believes.

W J Earle Introduction to Philosophy (1992) p 34

Something is deemed to be true if it fits in with the rest of our beliefs about the world that we already hold. Science works partly on coherence, as a scientific theory is deemed true when it fits in with other beliefs and theories.

Like the correspondence theory of truth, the **coherency theory** has been subject to criticism.

● Statements that do cohere are not necessarily true. There could be more than one coherent set of propositions, since there is nothing in the definition that demands 'that there is a unique most coherent set' (Dancy, *Introduction to Contemporary Epistemology*, page 113). Hence, at best, the theory provides necessary conditions for truth but not sufficient conditions.
● Truth becomes based on a truth bearer's relations to other truth bearers, rather than its relations to reality. This internalist criterion for

truth leads to relativism since many incompatible systems of belief may individually be internally consistent and self-supporting. Each individual system of belief could be held as the truth since it fits the criteria. It is an anti-realist approach.

● Does such a theory of truth hinder the likelihood of overturning a set of propositions that have formed a basic belief? Such a fundamental change of beliefs is called a paradigm shift, of which an illustration would be the Copernican revolutionary change from an earth-centred universe to a sun-centred universe. In a sense 'bliks' are like this. R M Hare used the illustration of an Oxford don who was convinced that all the other Oxford dons were trying to poison him. Any examples of behaviour that suggested differently were seen as a subtle attempt to put him off his guard. The problem is that nothing can count against it. It cannot be refuted by evidence because it helps to determine what counts as evidence.

4 The pragmatic theory

Statement *d* in the list on page 50, is often used as an example of the pragmatic theory. The quantum theory is regarded as a calculational tool rather than a description of reality. It is found to be an accurate predictor and so is deemed reliable to use. We call it true because it seems to work. Hence the pragmatic theory of truth has the focus on being practical. True propositions are those that 'work'. Acting on them and confirming them leads ultimately to positive results. It does not use the route of argument but prefers the test to be 'does it give us what we want from it?' A well-known supporter of this approach was William James (1842–1910) who argued that a successful scientific theory was judged on the basis of a connection between what is useful and what is true.

Criticisms raised against this approach include:

● This theory of the nature of truth is being confused with the criteria of truth. How we determine the truth of a proposition is different from what truth actually is.

● **Pragmatism** is not a reliable test for truth.

5 More recent approaches

In recent times the emphasis has moved away from theories of what truth is, and focussed instead on theories of what we are saying when we make truth assertions. The theories mentioned above, such as correspondence and coherence, are termed substantive theories of truth and all claim that truth is a property, i.e. X is true if and only if X has property P (such as corresponding to reality).

In contrast, these new approaches, called deflationary theories of truth, claim that there is no such property as truth. For instance, it is argued that by claiming something is true you are merely expressing agreement with other speakers. Deflationists regard classical theories of truth as 'attempting to analyse something which simply is not there' (*Concise Routledge Encyclopedia of Philosophy*, 2000).

Summary diagram Theories of truth

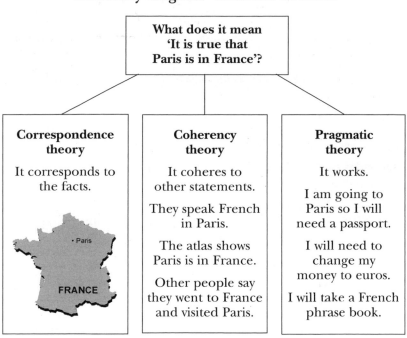

Answering questions on chapter 7

By the end of this chapter you should understand the three main theories of truth and the various criticisms of those theories.

A typical exam question would ask you to 'Identify two differences between the correspondence theory of truth and the coherency theory of truth'.

Clearly it would not be sufficient just to define the two theories. The focus is on identifying TWO differences. One difference that could be used is that one is realist and one is anti-realist. Can you find another difference?

This exam question measures the assessment objectives of knowledge and understanding and no more than about 100–150 words would be required if it was a part (a) question in the AS exam.

8 The Problem of Perception

KEY ISSUE To what extent do the images in our brain correspond to the objects outside of us in the world?

1 The problem

We live in the physical world, surrounded by matter. Indeed, we ourselves are made up of matter. But what is the nature of this physical world? We experience it through our senses but there is a gap between our experience and the object itself, since we experience the object as an image in our mind.

Objects can appear differently to different observers, or differently to the same observer under different conditions. A fly would receive information about the visual world completely differently from us, because of its compound eye. Try to list the ways a table in a room can appear differently to different people and under different conditions.

These are the kind of things that would make a difference: people diagnosed as colour blind; the light variation in the room; where you are standing in the room may change the look of the shape of the table; the feel of the texture of the table. If you were to ask a scientist about the table she would announce that there were more spaces between the atoms in the table than the space the atoms occupied.

She might also get you to look at the table under a microscope and examine its surface.

All these things bring into question the actual nature of matter. To what extent do the images in our brain correspond to the objects outside of us in the world? The table illustration is sufficient to make us unsure that the real is the same as what we immediately experience via our senses. Modern science now speaks in terms of neutrons and quarks that cannot be observed but are inferred. It seems that this element of reality is hidden from us.

A famous optical illusion depicting an old and young woman.

A further problem arises when we consider that our **perceptual** apparatus is not infallible. In chapter 3 we looked at everyday optical illusions such as railway lines that appear to meet as you look down the track. We can also experience illusions where we think we perceive things which are not in fact there at all (e.g. dreams).

2 Primary and secondary qualities

Philosophers have always been interested in the nature of reality. As far back as 400 BCE a Greek called Democritus concluded that the universe consists of very small particles moving in empty space (atoms literally means unsplittable). He argued that the atoms were different sizes but they all lacked colour/smell/taste. He said that these features only occurred when there were observers with eyes and noses.

This basic view became very popular again in the seventeenth century, favoured by people like Galileo and Boyle. A clear account can be found in John Locke's *Essay Concerning Human Understanding*. He divided the qualities to be found in bodies into two categories. The **primary qualities** are such things as extension, location, shape and number. These qualities are in objects whether we perceive the object or not. Qualities in the second group are called **secondary qualities** and are such things as colours, sounds, tastes and smells. These do not reside in the objects themselves but the power to produce them does. However this power is in the parts of objects that are too small to see. The power is in the object but the colour and sound exist only as sense-impressions. Both primary and secondary qualities produce ideas in our minds but the difference is that the qualities in objects that produce primary qualities are really like the ideas they produce, whilst the ideas produced by secondary qualities do not resemble the qualities that produced them. Primary qualities are inseparable from the object; there cannot be a body without a shape or size.

3 Descartes' wax illustration

Descartes would have roughly agreed with this view of primary and secondary qualities but would have argued that it was by rationalism (the mind) that we really knew the material objects and not by sensations. In *Meditation* 2, Descartes examined material objects, in particular a piece of wax. Originally he thought that he knew the wax was there because he saw it, felt it, smelt it. However, all the properties perceived by the senses change when the wax is melted. Descartes writes

> ...let it [the wax] be placed near the fire – what remained of the taste exhales, the smell evaporates, the colour changes, its figure is destroyed, its size increases, it becomes liquid, it grows hot, it can hardly be handled, and, although struck upon, it emits no sound. Does the same wax still remain after this change? It must be admitted that it does remain.

R Descartes *Meditation 2*

Descartes showed by this example that when he judged or inferred the wax was there, it was not based on what he sensed from his senses. The mind that contained the faculty of judgement was the source of his knowledge. He made a judgement that involved the use of concepts that were not drawn from experience. Sensations must be supplemented with judgements that use innate concepts – and this is how beliefs are formed about objects. The mind is required to perceive the wax.

This illustration is an important element in Descartes' *Meditations*. The illustration demonstrates:

- that empiricism is wrong in terms of being the foundation of knowledge
- that Descartes has identified what thinking involves
- that the basis of dualism has been identified (the mind is a thinking thing that takes on various thoughts whereas the body is an extended thing that takes on various shapes)
- that the new scientific world approach is consistent with rationalism rather than empiricism since it is the mind that arrives at a sound understanding of the physical world

In *Meditation 3–5* Descartes will show that belief in God is foundational to rationalism and the new science should not be seen as a threat to theism.

4 Naïve realism

What is the common sense view about perception? Try writing down three things that the average person would probably claim regarding perception. Possibly they would accept that there exists a world of material objects and that these objects exist whether or not we perceive them. Sense experience would presumably feature as the means of knowing the material objects, and they would probably conclude that the way we perceive the world is pretty much as it is.

Such a view is called **naïve realism**. It is 'naïve' in the sense of being simple, and it is 'realism' in the sense of claiming that there is an external world whose existence and nature is independent of us and our perception of it. The supporters of this view argue that objects have the properties they appear to have. Tastes, sounds and colours are not in the head of perceivers, they are qualities of the external objects that are perceived. If conditions are normal then red paint does have the property of being red. This view is also a form of direct realism in that the objects of immediate perception are external physical objects – there are no go-betweens necessary.

Can you think of any difficulties with this view? Look back at the problems on page 56 and consider whether any of those pose a problem for naïve realism/direct realism. Sense experience can be very illusionary; for instance, six pencil points touching a person's small of the back are sensed as only one. Naïve realism would compel us to wrongly conclude that there is only one pencil point. A similar form of attack came from A J Ayer (*The Foundations of Empirical Knowledge*, 1940) in which he used the example of the illusion of a stick in water that appears bent. The interesting feature is that there is no difference in the experience between the two parts of the stick that we see, yet only one is real. So the bent shape we are aware of can't be identical to the real stick. The bent shape is not a physical object. Ayer concludes that direct realism must therefore be wrong. For a detailed response to Ayer see *The Theory of Knowledge*, chapter 6. Ayer resolved the problem by developing a sense-datum theory, a form of representative realism.

5 Representative realism

One alternative to direct realism is indirect realism, also known as **representative realism**. This also favours an external world whose existence and nature is independent of us and our perception of it. However, the information acquired in perceiving an object is indirect. The immediate object of perception is a sensory experience that represents the object. Our perception of objects is mediated by our immediate perception of sensory experience. The question now arises as to whether this representation is accurate. Here representative realism divides. There is the common sense representative realism that says that our representations are accurate. Then there is another view which states that material objects do not possess all the properties they appear to possess. For instance, we see colour because of the reflected light waves of specific frequencies which cause us to superimpose colour. The object itself has no colour as such.

This second view is very close to those ideas held by Descartes and Locke involving primary and secondary qualities (page 57). The illusion of a stick in water that appears bent, is an illustration that has been used to support a sense-datum theory. The bent stick is not a physical object, but an illusion. We do not believe that the stick is bent even though it appears so. The experience of the bent stick is a mental state. That is what is meant by the term the 'sense-datum of the stick'. It is the sense-data that we are really aware of in cases of illusions. When I look at a stick, the stick causes my brain to be affected in certain ways, and this produces a sense-datum or image of the stick in my mind. What I am directly aware of is this sense-datum. The same is true of an actual stick. Therefore there is no difference between the two experiences, yet one is an illusion and one is real. It seems therefore that I cannot have direct experience of the physical object (since I cannot differentiate it from the illusion/mental experience) and what I must be experiencing in both cases is sense-datum.

Honderich (*Oxford Companion to Philosophy*, page 823) cites the example of a red elliptical sense-datum under the conditions of a red light and looking at an oblique angle. He claims that if you were clever, you could infer from the direct experience of that sense-datum that the cause is a white circle.

A useful task to make sure you understand the difference between physical objects and sense-data is to try and complete the following table.

Physical object	Sense data
Can sell or buy it	Cannot sell or buy it
Tables/chairs	Colours/smells/sounds/textures
Permanent	
Public	
	Immediate object of our experience
Can doubt	
Can exist unperceived	
	Directly perceived

A number of criticisms have been raised against the various forms of representative realism:

● Just because secondary qualities are nothing but a power to produce sensations, it does not mean that they are merely subjective. They could be genuine properties of the objects. For example, to be poisonous is simply power to produce a certain effect but it is a matter of clear fact whether something is poisonous.

● Secondary qualities may be defined in terms of their relationship to human perceivers, but properties that are relational can also be objective, e.g. being taller than another person is relational but it can also be a matter of fact.

● Secondary powers are said not to exist unperceived BUT they are powers so they could exist whether they were perceived or not. The Virgin Coke is sweet whether anyone tastes it or not.

● How can you know that the sense-data refers to real, 'out-there' objects? The theory seems to be circular in that it assumes that because the sense-datum is the colour blue then there exists an object in reality that is blue.

● Where is the sense-datum located? Is it produced by my brain?

6 Idealism

Perhaps the solution to representative realism is to accept that the only thing we have knowledge of is our own ideas. So why not believe that the only things that exist are minds and ideas? All that we experience are experiences of mental representations. Therefore the logical conclusion is that the external world is unknowable.

Such a radical view was proposed by Bishop Berkeley (1685–1753) and was called **idealism**. The name itself is slightly misleading and perhaps it is better described as idea-ism. He suggested that Locke was not vigorous enough. There is no way to distinguish between primary and secondary qualities. All qualities are secondary and subjective since even so-called primary qualities are all qualities 'in my head'. Knowledge is based on our experience, and our experience is of ideas. So how can we infer the existence of anything beyond our ideas? We must conclude that there is no evidence for the existence of things outside the mind (the external world). Berkeley also argued that since all we can perceive by sense are ideas, then if it is claimed that we perceive physical objects by sense, those physical objects must consist of ideas. Hence Berkeley eliminated material substances.

People's usual reaction to this approach is to dismiss it out of hand. To dismiss the real world seems against common sense. However, before you do, try this little exercise. Try to imagine a house with no one perceiving it. To imagine a house unperceived by anyone seems easy, until you realise that you are perceiving it, and hence the house is not unperceived. You can see why Berkeley coined the phrase *esse est percipi* which means 'to be, is to be perceived'. Sense experiences cannot exist unexperienced.

So how did he explain something as basic as an apple? Objects are groups of ideas (sensations). An apple has sweet sensations along with green sensations, along with hard sensations, along with juicy sensations. The whole collection of those ideas are what we call an apple. Language organises ideas into physical objects. But our experiences appear to be consistent with the experience of (supposed) other people. Also things appear to exist continuously rather than come and go suddenly when they are not being perceived. Berkeley accounted for this by appealing to the existence of God. It is God who is always perceiving all things. He created the sense-data and minds to perceive them. God gives us sense experiences that are orderly. In this theory of perception Berkeley was reaffirming empiricism since experience was the basis for knowledge. The theory also reinstated the need for God that the views of Locke seemingly no longer required. Finally, it removed the scepticism of empiricism.

Not surprisingly idealism has attracted critical scrutiny. Some key criticisms are listed below:

● If other people exist, are they ideas only (since Berkeley rejected material substance)? Indeed, in what sense can I be perceived by others?
● The theory requires the existence of God. But how can you know there is a God? To appeal to the order of the sense-data seems a circular argument
● Descartes had earlier argued that if you can know there is a God, then you could know there are physical objects. So shouldn't Berkeley accept the notion of physical objects?
● Not being able to know whether objects exist is not the same thing as knowing physical objects do not exist
● Not being able to perceive without a mind is not the same thing as knowing that what you perceive cannot exist without a mind

● Not the best possible hypothesis
● What about the evil demon deceiving us about ideas?

7 Phenomenalism

Phenomenalism is a theory of perception popularised by the logical positivist movement. Logical positivists claimed that for a statement to be meaningful it had to be verifiable by the sense experiences. To understand a proposition means to know what is the case if it is true. Clearly physical objects cannot be known directly and so cannot be verified. The solution is to translate all talk about physical objects into talk about possible sense experiences, which can be verified since they are direct experiences. In this approach, matter is seen as a logical construction out of sense experience. To say that matter is a logical construct of experience is to say that everything using physical matter vocabulary may be said in a more basic or fundamental way referring only to sense experience. A J Ayer (*Language, Truth and Logic*, 1971) is particularly associated with this view called linguistic phenomenalism. To check that you understand this theory about perception, try translating the statement 'There is a green chair by the window' into sense experience statements (see end of chapter for answer).

The attraction of this approach is that it resolves the problem of identifying the nature or existence of physical things, since translation into sense-datum makes the statement a certainty (you can't deny having those sense experiences). Equally resolved is the problem of knowing if physical objects remain whilst you are not perceiving them. Such statements can be translated into 'If you went into the next room, you would be aware of such and such sense-datum'.

Criticisms:

● Contemporary philosophy tends to argue that sense experience is a logical construct from the actual physical world, rather than the other way around.
● How can anyone be sure that they have listed sufficient sense-datum to secure uniqueness of reference?
● Do such statements about sense-data allow for delusions and dreams, where there is no real world object that exists yet the sense experiences do?
● Objects exist unperceived whilst sense-data do not.

By the end of this chapter you should understand the problem posed by perception and the various theories that have been proposed. You should also be able to critically assess those theories

The completed table from page 61 is:

Physical object	Sense data
Can sell or buy it	Cannot sell or buy it
Tables/chairs	Colours/smells/sounds/textures
Permanent	Temporary – exists only as long as we are perceiving it
Public	Private
Inferred from sense-data	Immediate object of our experience
Can doubt	Cannot doubt
Can exist unperceived	Cannot exist unperceived
Indirectly perceived	Directly perceived

The statement 'There is a green chair by the window' (page 63) can be translated into a statement such as 'There is a chair-like datum together with a green-like datum and they are both next to a window-like datum'. This could be expanded upon, for instance, by breaking down the 'chair-like datum' into particular shape, texture datum etc. If you want to read Ayer's account then look at chapter 3 in his book *Language Truth and Logic*. In a later book *The Problem of Knowledge*, Ayer was rather more critical of this approach.

A typical question on this topic might be 'Identify two similarities and two differences between naïve realism and representative realism'.

One similarity is that they are both types of realism and so claim that the physical world exists independently of perception. Both also claim that the material world is the source of their perception experience.

One obvious difference is that naïve realism claims that we perceive things directly, whereas representative realism claims it is indirect. Also, naïve realism holds that what we experience resembles the physical object. Representative realism accepts the possibility that the experience may not resemble the physical object.

9 The Scope of Knowledge

KEYWORDS

Cartesian – an adjective derived from the Latin name of Descartes

essence – an object's nature

external world – the idea of an objective real world

formal reality – the level of reality of an object

inductive inference – a conclusion that is supported, but not proven, from the premises

objective reality – the level of reality of the object that it represents

ontological – concerned with 'being'

KEY ISSUE In chapters 3 and 4 we considered rationalism and empiricism as a basis for a systematic account of human knowledge. This chapter will consider the specific areas of knowledge of the **external world**, the past and induction.

1 The external world

a) The problem

The term 'external world' refers to all those objects and events which exist external to and independent of perceivers. This includes not just tables and chairs but also other perceivers. The problem posed by philosophy is 'how can a person gain knowledge of the external world?' At its most sceptical, it questions whether any knowledge can be gained of the external world. In some ways, the last chapter on perception was addressing a similar issue. There we looked at the traditional accounts of our perception of the external world. Direct realism states that the physical world is as it is perceived, and we perceive it directly. Representative realism argues that the external world causes our sensations. Idealism rejected the notion of a physical world and phenomenalism claimed that all talk of the external world should be translated into talk about sense-data.

It would be useful to recap on the various reasons why we might be doubtful about our knowledge of the external world. As mentioned above, we are aware that there is a gap between the external world and our experience of it. The various theories of perception were partly an attempt to resolve this problem. This suggests that we cannot be sure what causes our sense experience. In addition, we can experience illusions, hallucinations or dreams. These can make us believe we are experiencing the real external world, when in fact we are not. Moreover, science informs us that it takes about eight minutes for the sun's light to reach us. This means that when we see the sun we are seeing it as it was eight minutes ago. We are seeing the past. Indeed, what we are seeing may no longer exist. If these doubts were not enough, Descartes introduced his methodological device – the evil demon. It was the fact that this evil demon could be deceiving us about everything, including the actual existence of an external world, that brought total scepticism about the external world.

b) Descartes' solution

It should be noted that those who are not studying Descartes as a set text do not require the detail that this section contains.

In *Meditations*, Descartes argues that we can reason that the external world actually exists and in approximately the form that we think it does. At the initial stage of his argument, Descartes uses two arguments to establish the existence of God. These can be found in *Meditations 3* and 5. They are known respectively as the trademark argument and the **ontological** argument. In *Meditations 1–2* Descartes established the certainty that he existed. This was discussed in chapter 3 where we examined rationalism (page 21). To progress to other knowledge, Descartes has to address the problem of the evil demon, so he focuses on the idea of an omnipotent perfect being. He intends to show that God exists as a perfect being, who could create the external world (about which we have clear and distinct ideas) and, being perfect, he would not deceive us. Therefore what our senses lead us to believe must exist, otherwise God would be deceiving us.

i The trademark argument

Descartes argues that our idea of perfection is related to its perfect origin, namely God, in a similar way that a trademark, or logo is put onto an article of work by its maker. The argument itself relies heavily on medieval philosophy similar to that used by Aquinas (1225–1274). Descartes regarded the highest form of reality as something that was not causally dependent on anything for its existence. That which showed dependency was of a lesser form of reality. He then adopted two principles:

1   every object has a cause
2   there must be at least as much reality in the cause as in the effect of that cause.

These two principles are then applied to the idea of a perfect being. Descartes concludes that this idea of a perfect being must come from a self-dependent substance (a reality of the highest order) and this is what we call God. It might be argued that the idea of God could have been caused by another idea or by a created substance. This would still satisfy his two principles. However, in Descartes' philosophy the cause must be equal to or higher than whatever the effect represents. Technically this is expressed by the principle that a cause must have at least as much **formal reality** as the effect has **objective reality**. By formal reality Descartes meant the level of reality it had. By objective reality he meant the level of reality of the thing it represents. Put simply, if the idea is of a perfect being, then its cause must derive from something that shares the same level of reality or higher. However, the perfect being is of the highest level of reality already (a self-dependent substance). Hence Descartes concludes that the idea of a perfect being must derive from a perfect being. Therefore God exists.

This is not an easy argument to follow and it may well be worth reading it again, and this time noting down any weaknesses you find with the argument.

The weaknesses stem mostly from the argument being based on medieval philosophy and ideas. For example:

- Is it true that every event has a cause?
- Is the idea of a hierarchy of realities reasonable?
- Is it true that there must be at least as much reality in the cause as in the effect of that cause?
- Is it true that the cause must have at least as much formal reality as the effect has objective reality?
- Regardless of medieval philosophy, doesn't the argument collapse on the grounds that the evil demon could be deceiving him about the logic of his argument?

ii The ontological argument

This is a form of argument that was originally presented by Anselm (1033–1109). 'Ontological' literally means 'concerned with being'. Descartes presents this argument in *Meditation 5*.

God, a supremely perfect being, has all perfections
Existence is a perfection
Therefore God, a supremely perfect being, exists.

This argument focussed on the idea of **essence**. In medieval philosophy, you first of all considered a being's essence, and then decided whether the actual being existed or not. The essence is the thing's nature, or that without which it could not be what it is. Descartes argued that when you examined the essence of the perfect being, one part of it was existence itself. Existence is an aspect of perfection. The conclusion therefore was that God must exist.

In *Meditation 5* Descartes answers a number of objections that were voiced about this argument.

- **Objection 1**: Essence is separate from existence.
  As mentioned above, medieval philosophy saw these as two different questions. However, Descartes points out that there are some qualities that an object necessarily had. He uses the example of a triangle that must have three angles adding up to 180 degrees. Equally the notion of a slope demands the idea of a valley. In the same way, existence cannot be separated from the concept of God. If God is thought of as containing all perfections, then existence is one of those perfections.
- **Objection 2**: Thinking it doesn't make it exist.
  Descartes agrees with that view. However, he points out that the necessity of God's existence imposes on our thoughts not the reverse!
- **Objection 3**: A false supposition will lead to a false conclusion.
  Descartes quotes the illustration of a circle that is claimed can inscribe (place within it) all quadrilateral figures. Since a rhombus is a quadrilateral figure then it would conclude that a circle could inscribe a rhombus. It should be noted that a rhombus cannot be inscribed in a circle. Although the form of the argument is deductive, the first premise is false and this leads to the conclusion being false. The claim is that Descartes' use of the premise 'a supremely perfect being has all perfections' is being claimed as equally invalid and so leads to a wrong conclusion that God exists. Descartes replies that the analogy is invalid. In the case of the circle, when he thinks about that, he has no clear and distinct idea that it is necessarily true. Indeed it is false, and so it is no wonder that the conclusion reached from it is false. However, when he thinks of the supremely perfect being, he clearly and distinctly perceives that it is necessarily true and the conclusion drawn from it is true.

iii Criticisms of the ontological argument

Descartes' ontological argument raises the issue about his use of ' a clear and distinct idea'. On the basis of the certainty of the cogito, he concludes that clear and distinct ideas are a test for something being true. In *Meditations*, Descartes does not really define what he means by a clear and distinct idea. However, his other writings imply that it is the intellectual equivalent to visual perception of an object under good conditions, i.e. we can discriminate the object from its environment and make out each of its parts. Indeed, it is so clear and obvious that it cannot be doubted. The mind cannot help assenting to it.

It is at this point that philosophers have accused Descartes of arguing in a circle (the **Cartesian** circle).

- Our clear and distinct idea about reality is true because God doesn't deceive
- We know God exists because we have a clear and distinct idea about God
- Therefore circular argument since it uses as part of the argument the very thing it is claiming to prove.

The problem is showing that clear and distinct ideas are reliable without appealing to God's existence. Descartes himself admits in *Meditation 3* that he cannot be sure that such ideas are always reliable. He acknowledges that he needs God's existence to guarantee that clear and distinct ideas lead to truth.

The ontological argument for God's existence has also been challenged on a number of other grounds. One of the major opponents to the argument was Immanuel Kant. Kant made the point that existence is not a real predicate. That is, it does not tell us what an object is like (a quality or characteristic). Kant felt that 'exist' was a word that merely stated that a concept had an actuality. It didn't actually add anything to the concept (i.e. make it more perfect). The real contains no more than the merely possible, so a concept is not made more perfect by adding reality. Kant expressed it like this:

> If we take the subject (God) with all its predicates (e.g. all knowledge), and say 'God is' or 'There is a God', we attach no new predicate to the concept of God … merely posit it as being an object that stands in relation to my concept. The content of both must be one and the same …The real contains no more than the merely possible. A hundred real thalers do not contain the least coin more than a hundred possible thalers.
>
> I Kant *The Critique of Pure Reason* (1781)

Brian Davies has expressed the same point using a different example.

> For someone who claims to compare two things, one of which exists and the other of which does not, is just not doing what he says he is doing. If we contrast (or compare) A with B, then both A and B must exist. A non-existent book is not different from a real book. Nor is it similar. It is just not there to be either similar or different to anything. Hence as Kant said 'Being' is the positing of a thing.
>
> B Davies *Thinking about God* (1985) p 107

We do not add anything to the concept when we declare that it 'is'. Otherwise it would not be exactly the same thing that exists but something more than we had thought in the concept; and we could not, therefore, say that the exact object of my concept exists.

Thus many regard 'exists' more as a number. To say that something exists is to deny the number zero. Bertrand Russell made a similar point. He used the example of 'cows exist' but 'unicorns do not exist'. He said that we are not talking about cows and saying that they have the attribute of existence or that unicorns lack this attribute. Rather we are talking of concepts of a cow and a unicorn and saying that one of them has an existence and one of them does not.

However, supporters of the ontological argument have responded to such criticisms, arguing that existence can be a real predicate. Stephen Davis notes that:

Of the real hundred thalers, my concept of them includes the property of having-purchasing-power-in-the-real-world. My concept of a hundred thalers does not have that property.

S Davis *God, Reason and Theistic Proofs* (1997) p 35

Another attack on the ontological argument has been focussed on the fact that 'God exists' seems to be an analytic proposition about existence. Many philosophers argue that propositions about existence are not analytic but synthetic and contingent. If this is correct then any argument that derives from an existential analytic proposition, must be in error. Hence the ontological argument must be flawed in some way.

In reply supporters of the ontological argument have argued that IT IS possible to have analytic existential propositions. They cite such examples as 'A number greater than a million exists' and 'Science Fiction characters do not exist' as analytic existential propositions. The debate continues ...!

Even if one were to accept that existence was a perfection, some philosophers still feel that the argument fails. This is because the thrust of the ontological argument seems to be that by defining God you can be assured of its existence. To most, such an idea seems absurd. It implies you can define anything into existence. There seems to be some intellectual sleight of hand involved in moving from a definition to proving an existence. Many feel that filling out a concept and showing that there really is something to which the concept refers, are two quite different processes and the first does NOT lead to the second. Remember that the ontological argument alleges that we cannot explain the concept of God properly without coming to the conclusion that he exists. Hence it implies that it is a contradiction to deny the existence of God.

Kant proposed that no such contradiction arose if you rejected both subject and predicate 'for nothing is left that you can contradict.' Kant expressed it in these words:

It would be self-contradictory to posit a triangle and yet reject its three angles, but there is no contradiction in rejecting the triangle together with its three angles.

I Kant *Critique of Pure Reason* (1781)

Definitions only tell us what God would be like IF he existed. It cannot establish whether he does in fact exist. One can move from a concept of imagination to a concept of reality but not from a concept of imagination to reality. Hence there is no contradiction in denying the reality of a conceptual being who has all perfections. When we say that existence is part of God's definition, we are merely saying that no non-existing being can be God. To put it another way, if God exists he will have all perfections, but it is not a contradiction to say that such a concept does not have an actuality.

Hume said:

> However much our concept of an object may contain, we must go outside of it to determine whether or not it exists. We cannot define something into existence – even if it has all the perfections we can imagine.

> D Hume *Dialogues Concerning Natural Religion* (1779)

You've guessed it – this view has not gone unchallenged. Some people have pointed out that explaining a concept can make non-existence apparent. Take for example 'round squares'. These cannot exist. A concept leads to a non-existence. So perhaps the two processes of concept and actuality are related and therefore PERHAPS it is possible by filling out a concept that you can move to actuality. All very teasing. Hence the debate continues.

c) Russell's common sense view

The rationalists had tried to bridge the gap between mental states and the external world, by *a priori* propositions. In contrast, Bertrand Russell *Problems of Philosophy* (1912) argues for a common sense view about the existence of the external world. He gives a number of illustrations to argue that our sense-data are signs of physical objects. For instance, if a cloth completely hides a table, we could not receive any sense-data from the table. Yet the tablecloth remains in place, suggesting that the table exists independently of our seeing it.

Equally the fact that many people share the same object suggests there is a common existing object independent of the people. He uses the illustration of ten people sitting round a dinner table. They see the same tablecloth, knives, forks, spoons and glasses from different perspectives suggesting there are public neutral objects over and above their private sense-data. The changes that are seen in objects are predictable from laws of perspective and reflection of light. Also similar sense data are experienced by different people at different times. Here Russell uses the illustration of someone buying a table from someone else and collecting it sometime later.

Russell admits that it is impossible to prove the existence of things other than ourselves and our experiences, but he argues that to regard the whole of life as a dream, though not impossible, is less simple than the common sense view. He again illustrates how this view of simplicity seems a much easier view and makes good sense of our experiences. He uses the example of a cat that goes in and out of a room. To imagine that it only exists when I see it would seem absurd, as would an account of its hunger. From our own experience we know appetites grow, so it is not unreasonable to argue that the same is true of the cat and so it must exist in the gap when we do not see it.

Russell considers that our beliefs may be mistaken. However, the reason for rejecting them would have to be based on some other belief, and having established an orderly and coherent relationship of beliefs about the external world, it seems more pragmatic to accept this view as true.

2 The past

a) Recent past

Interestingly, most people can remember what they were doing on September 11 2001, when they heard that the World Trade Centre in New York had been attacked. However, can you remember what you were doing 6 years ago today? What about 6 months ago or even 6 days ago? Try to list how you would determine what you were doing.

I expect that checking with other people's memories will be an important method of finding out. Certainly knowledge about the experienced recent past involves relying on our own memory and others' memories, but both are fallible. We are aware that memory is selective, edited and can be repressed. We seem to have the ability to create and distort the past and come to sincerely believe that distortion. Hypnosis, however, suggests that events forgotten remain in our subconscious. Certainly memories play an important part in our lives. Indeed, memory is the condition of personal identity. It gives us an 'inner story' and is essential for the concept of the 'I'. But it is not always possible to tell the difference between memory and imagination. Hume (*Enquiries Concerning Human Understanding*, 1748) identifies the distinction between the two as one of relative 'liveliness, force and vivacity' of the experiences. However, it is possible that an imagination experience is more vivid than a memory one.

Bertrand Russell recognised the problem of knowledge about the recent past, and argued that perhaps the world came into being five minutes ago and our memories are not real memories at all. Like Hume, he tried to identify the qualitative element of a memory image and said that memory images are accompanied by a feeling of familiarity.

Some appeal to cross-checking as a means of validating remembered events. This might involve asking whether a person was in a position to remember the event. Could they have known about it in some other way? The weakness with this is that it is cross-checking one memory experience against another, so provides no grounds for the reliability of memory.

Positive arguments for reliable memory include the use of language. Our language is dependent on memory, for how else could we be sure that we are using the words correctly? Others point to the concept of forgetting. Forgetting only has meaning if it is accepted that sometimes memory is correct.

b) Distant past

When the past is beyond a living memory then appeal has to be made to written materials, oral tradition and artefacts. The problem here is the testing for authenticity, which raises a whole range of issues, e.g. the sources of the written material, their independence, the possible bias of the writers, how far the sources cohere and support each other. Artefacts also need interpreting and account given of their number and significance.

Hume's chapter on miracles in *Enquiries concerning Human Understanding* (ch. 10) is an interesting study of assessing testimony.

3 The future

Certainty concerning events that are still in the future seems unknowable. For instance, no one knows what the winning lottery numbers are for next Saturday. However, there are events that people would generally regard as certain that are still in the future. Can you think of any?

Consider the following:

a   If I let go of my pen, then it will drop to the floor.
b   The sun will rise tomorrow.
c   The billiard ball will roll when hit by another billiard ball.

It would be reasonable to argue that these events will happen. What they all share in common is the principle of **inductive inference**. Put simply, the principle states that the future will resemble the past. More specifically, this principle involves drawing conclusions about the general case from the particular case. If all *observed* As are followed by Bs, then it is inferred that all future As will be followed by Bs. For example, it has always been *observed* that billiard balls have rolled when struck by another billiard ball. Therefore we should expect in the future that the billiard ball will roll when struck by another billiard ball. This principle involves observing a number of particular events and inferring that all such events will be the same. In a similar way, if all observed As are Bs then all As are Bs. For example, if all *observed* swans are white, then it is inferred that all swans are white. It is inductive since even if the premise is true it is possible that the conclusion is false. For instance, Captain Cook found black swans in Australia, but up until that time it was thought that all swans were white.

Philosophers have identified various problems posed by the principle of inductive inference. One of the classic statements of the problem was given by Hume (*Enquiry Concerning Human Understanding*), in which he argued that such beliefs were not based on any reasoning but 'a certain instinct of our nature'. He was aware that it is a circular argument to claim that nature is uniform, because we need to assume it true in order to demonstrate it true. This led to Hume's scepticism since the principle led only to a probability.

This implies that the view of rationality as a process demanding deductive reasoning is an inadequate definition. A J Ayer argued in a similar fashion (*Language, Truth and Logic*) stating that using the past as a guide to the future is part of what is meant by acting rationally. Bertrand Russell (*The Problems of Philosophy*) rejected certainty, pointing out that not only did it involve a circular argument but that we could never be sure we have discovered a law that does not have exceptions.

However, he gave a number of arguments to support the principle:

- The belief in the uniformity of nature is the belief that everything that has happened or will happen is an instance of some general law to which there are NO exceptions. Science seems to support this, in that any general law that had an exception has been replaced by a general law that embraces that exception. Therefore uniformity does exist. However, even if this is true, it is no guarantee that the law will work tomorrow.

- The future can be verified. From the perspective of yesterday, today was future. Hence that which was future has now become the past. Therefore we have experience of the future and the principle can be tested. However, it does not verify the future futures, since they may disprove the principle.

- The inductive principle cannot be disproved by appeals to experience. Russell uses the example of seeing only white swans. Such data makes it probable that all swans are white. Even if some are black, it doesn't disprove the induction theory. Merely that the person should have taken into account that colour is a very variable characteristic in species of animals and so probability on such a basis is risky. Probability is always relative to data. Hence there may be some data not taken into account that would radically change the probability, if the data were known.

- The principle of induction has worked in daily life and in science. Therefore it is pragmatic to use it. If a truth about the future is to be known then the inductive procedure is probably the best guide.

- Other philosophers have also questioned the extent to which freewill is compatible with knowing the future, though this is more focussed on human action than scientific laws.

Summary diagram

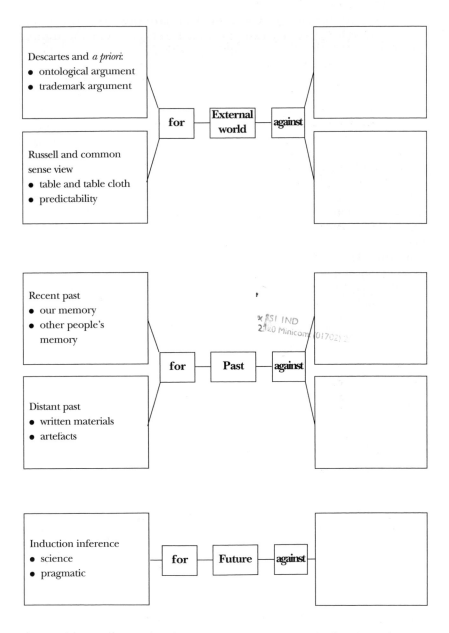

Using the structure above, list the arguments against in the empty boxes.

Answering questions on chapter 9

By the end of this chapter you should understand the problem of gaining knowledge of the external world, the past and the future (induction). You should also be able to critically assess the solutions suggested to those problems.

Bertrand Russell's book (*The Problems of Philosophy*) is recommended reading, especially chapters 1–4.

Exam questions based around the contents of these chapters could include material already covered in previous chapters. For instance discussion about the external world lends itself to discussion about knowledge as well as scepticism. Material from Descartes' *Meditations* would also be relevant.

Examiners' reports are useful sources for advice on answering exam questions. One of the frequent comments appearing in them is that candidates tend to spend far too long on introductory issues. The examiners are awarding marks for arguing a point in a sustained manner and the inclusion of a rhetorical question is not an adequate substitute. The material in this chapter contains illustrative examples. Again, it should be noted that examples do not speak for themselves and the point of the illustration needs stating. There is always the danger that the vivid reciting of the illustration becomes the main part of the answer.

A typical question might be 'To what extent, if at all, do we have knowledge of future events?'

The trigger 'to what extent' immediately flags up the fact that the question is assessing evaluative skills. One approach is to identify the difficulties of having knowledge of the future. This will involve discussions about both induction and the criteria necessary for knowledge. For the higher level marking you would have to respond to those difficulties highlighted and argue that possibly a pragmatic approach is reasonable with appeals to such things as 'past futures'. However, whether it ultimately can fulfil the knowledge criteria may well depend on what one regards as 'justifiable'.

10 Descartes' *Meditations*
(an appendix on Cartesian dualism)

KEY ISSUE Throughout this book, various material contained in Descartes' *Meditations* have been discussed. This chapter examines the remaining material not yet covered, which centres on the arguments for **Cartesian dualism**. The book is therefore useful for those wishing to study *Meditations* as the set philosophical text.

The material which has so far been examined can be found on the following pages:

Meditation 1 – method of doubt and distrust of senses (pages 20)
Meditation 2 – cogito (see pages 21)
              – illustration of the wax (pages 58)
Meditation 3 – trademark argument (pages 66)
              – clear and distinct ideas (pages 68)
Meditation 5 – ontological argument (pages 67)

The remaining material (apart from Meditation 4) is mainly concerned with Descartes' theories regarding the relationship between mind and body.

1 The 'I'

In *Meditation 2*, having established the cogito, Descartes asks what the 'I' is. He concludes that it is a thinking thing.

> It is a thing that doubts, understands [conceives], affirms, denies, wills, refuses, that imagines also, and perceives.

> R Descartes *Meditation 2*

Descartes regards thinking as an experience of one's own mind. He previously had viewed humans in an Aristotelian way. According to Aristotle, humans were defined as rational animals, that consisted of a body and a soul. The activities of the soul were seen to include eating, moving around, sense perception and thought. According to Aristotle, the soul is what makes a thing alive; it is the principle of life. For Descartes, consciousness is the key feature of the mind, not intellect. However, the soul and the body were thought to form a single substance. It is true that Plato had favoured a dualistic view but Descartes gave forceful new arguments for the dualistic model. Together with his argument about the wax, he had indicated that the universe could consist of two different substances. Firstly mind, defined as a thinking thing that takes on various thoughts and is unextended. Secondly, body (matter) which is **extended** (3D) and takes on various shapes.

By the end of *Meditation 2* it must be admitted that Descartes has not proven Cartesian dualism, since he admits that it is possible that the 'I' may also include the body. Descartes also acknowledges that because of the evil deceiver he cannot know whether he has a body and therefore the only certainty he has at this point (*Meditation 2*) is that he is a thing that thinks. It is in *Meditation 6* that he attempts to prove that mind and body are different substances and that both exist.

Hume later challenged the Cartesian view that thoughts were properties of the self. He argued that he could find no such awareness of a self. Instead he regarded thoughts as individual objects in their own right. Selves were simply bundles of such objects.

2 Arguments for the material world

In *Meditation 6* Descartes gives some inductive arguments for the existence of the material world.

a) Imagination and understanding

The steps of this argument are:

● it is possible to imagine a triangle and understand it
● it is possible to understand a **chilliogan** as a 1000 sided figure but it is NOT possible to imagine it

- this implies that understanding is distinct from imagination
- imagination turns upon the object whilst intellect turns upon itself and contemplates one of the ideas contained within itself
- imagination does not seem a necessary part of my essence.

Therefore, imagination is best accounted for by the existence of an external body.

b) Passive perception

The steps of this argument are:

- ideas appear against my will
- the faculty that achieves this must be in the substance not my will
- this substance must have reality either in God or an external extended body
- God does not deceive.

Therefore perceptions probably come from an external extended body otherwise God would be deceiving me into thinking they come from an external extended body.

Probably the most damaging criticism against this argument is Descartes' failure to prove that there exists a perfect God. For criticisms of Descartes' arguments for God see pages 67–71. It is therefore possible that Descartes' sensory experiences are produced by an evil deceiver or by some other way.

3 Arguments for Cartesian dualism

Descartes argued for **substance dualism** since he viewed the universe as containing two distinct substances – the mind(soul) and the material world. He saw humans as composed of these two substances which interacted with each other. Hence his view of the mind/body relationship was called **interactionism**. In *Meditation 6* he used two arguments to prove substance dualism.

a) Separability

The steps of this argument are:

- I have a clear and distinct understanding of myself as a conscious, but not extended thing
- I have a clear and distinct understanding of my body as an extended, but not a conscious thing
- whatever is clear and distinct can be brought about by God
- my body and mind can therefore exist separately.

Therefore I am distinct from my body and my bodily features are not essential to my existence.

Criticisms against this argument focus on the fact that if two concepts are distinct it does not necessarily entail that they exist separately from one another. For example, shape and colour are conceptually distinct but shape cannot exist without colour. Therefore Descartes is wrong to conclude that because mind and body are conceptually distinct they can exist separately.

Another criticism is that a body (e.g. the brain) may be required for the thinking to take place. In addition, the fact that God has the power to create mind and body separately, does not mean that he has exercised that power.

b) Indivisibility

The steps of this argument are:

● the mind is indivisible whilst the body is divisible

Therefore the mind must be of an entirely different nature from the body.

Keith Maslin points out that the

> concepts of divisibility and indivisibility have no application to mental states and capacities, owing to the fact that these are not logical substances, things capable of existing in their own right.

> K Maslin *An Introduction to the Philosophy of Mind* (2001) p 64

It is not meaningful to speak about mental states and experiences being cut in half.

Some have argued that perhaps the mind is divisible since Descartes himself lists a number of faculties of the mind (e.g. it doubts, understands, affirms). Indeed recent work on dividing the brain suggests that the mind can also be divided. For a discussion on this see chapter 8 in Peter Carruthers' book *Introducing Persons* (Routledge, 1986).

4 Interactionism

Dualism is often expressed as saying that mind and matter are different substances. Substance does not mean a chemical substance but a 'basic constituent of reality'. As noted above, Descartes' view of the mind/body relationship was interactionism based on substance dualism. This is in contrast to **property dualism**. In property dualism the mind is dependent on the brain and is a property of it. If the brain is destroyed so would be the mind. In contrast, substance dualism is claiming that mind and body are not dependent and one can survive without the other – they are two different substances.

Dualistic interactionism holds that a person is a composite being consisting of a mental object (a spirit-like immaterial mind) joined with a material body. Further, these two entities causally interact, i.e. they causally affect each other. This experience of interaction is something we all feel. For instance, my desire for a drink causes me to move my body to the kitchen. Likewise my dry throat is part of the desire for a drink.

Descartes thought that the soul operated through the pineal gland since it was sensitive, middle of brain and singular (not repeated in each hemisphere). Keith Maslin (*An Introduction to the Philosophy of Mind*, page 46f) describes the Cartesian view in terms of the mind (soul) giving the pineal gland a tiny push which was magnified by a chain of physical causes and effects, ending in bodily movement. The nerves were like fine tubes containing 'animal spirits' – NOT ghosts of departed animals but highly rarefied blood. The eyes projected images on the surface of the pineal gland and 'seeing' consisted in the soul attending to the image (remember the wax illustration on page 58).

Descartes said the relationship between mind and body was NOT like a pilot and a boat but rather more tightly bound so they formed a unit. Hence we can actually feel pain rather than just perceiving it. He called this intermingling of soul and body – 'substantial union'.

5 Problems with interactionism

a) Where does interactionism take place?

For interactionists such as Descartes the interaction takes place literally in the brain. Descartes thought that the pineal gland in the brain (one of the few non-paired parts of the brain) was the connecting link. In more recent times this location is regarded as wrong since the pineal gland does not seem to be affected by all the brain processes which affect the mind. Indeed, dualistic interactionism requires that mental events be located in the brain, but at the same time denies that mental events have a location.

In reply, the dualist would argue that it is an assumption that two events that causally interact must both have a spatial location. Hence this is not a fatal objection though it does lessen the likelihood of dualistic interactionism.

b) How can interactionism take place?

If mental and physical events have different kinds of causal abilities, how can they interact? For instance, physical forces causally affect the material. Mental events do not have mass or location and so cannot exert a physical force. Thus interaction between the mental and the physical cannot take place. Basically the mental does not have the capability to interact and a similar argument applies to the physical.

The response of the dualist is to argue that all that is required is that both of them are 'events'. We cannot state *a priori* that minds and brains cannot interact. True, they may not interact in the way we ordinarily understand causation, but it does not logically follow that they therefore can't interact. Indeed studies in parapsychology suggest some evidence for the mind being able to affect the physical (e.g. moving objects). Hypnosis and psychosomatic illnesses seem evidence for causal interaction.

c) Interactionism violates the conservation of energy principle

The principle of the conservation of energy states that the amount of energy in a closed physical system remains constant. However this seems to contradict interaction dualism because when a physical event takes place energy is transferred. But the physical energy involved in the bodily event is not transferred to anything else yet energy is lost. Hence the law is broken. The conclusion is that interactionism is not true.

In reply, C D Broad, a twentieth-century dualist, argues that physical energy may not be required to bring about a mental event, because mental phenomena involve no physical energy. With regard to the mental affecting the physical, Broad suggests that the mental event changes the direction of the nerve impulse by changing resistance at **synapses**, and it is the relative levels of resistance that cause nerve currents to take various routes. This redistribution does not cause any change in the total amount of energy. Thus in both cases of interaction, the energy principle is NOT violated.

d) God deceives us

This problem is raised by Descartes in *Meditation 6* and his solution is known as Descartes' **theodicy**. He notes that sometimes our mind tells us things that are wrong. We appear to be deceived. For instance, those who are ill may desire a drink which may aggravate the illness, as in the case of dropsy. Surely a good God would prevent nature from deceiving us?

His solution centres on the argument that the body produces just one sensation in the mind and this is the one that preserves the body the most (thirst/health). The body works like a cord, so that when it is pulled at one point the effect would be the same had it been pulled at a different point. As a result we can be wrong about the origin of our sensations. However, this is the best system possible and God gives us faculties to know when it is wrong so we can correct it. God is no deceiver as mistakes only happen when we do not make the effort to contemplate thoroughly. Once again Descartes emphasises the importance of the mind.

6 Descartes' contribution

Many feel that Descartes produced a compromise between the Church and the new science of his age. The two distinct substances of mind and body provided a compromise between the powerful new science with its mechanistic, deterministic laws of motion of physical bodies, and the powerful Church with its teachings of a perfect spiritual being, immune from determinism and the laws of physics. Truth for science involved investigating mechanistic laws. Truth for the Church involved revelation, the souls of humans and the freedom of the mind. Descartes' influence dominated the Western world and its philosophy.

Summary diagram of Descartes' *Meditations*

Meditation 1	method of doubt illusion argument dream argument evil demon argument
Meditation 2	cogito the 'I' wax illustration
Meditation 3	clear and distinct idea trademark argument
Meditation 4	clear and distinct ideas are true the nature of error
Meditation 5	ontological argument
Meditation 6	imagination and understanding passive perception Cartesian dualism interactionism theodicy

Answering questions on chapter 10

By the end of this chapter you should understand the arguments that Descartes uses to prove the existence of the material world and substance dualism. You should also be able to critically assess these arguments as well as being able to discuss the problems of interactionism.

The questions set at AS level on Descartes are based around the text of *Meditations*. It is vital that candidates have a thorough knowledge of the text. One danger is that candidates' answers are too general and unfocussed. It should be noted that very specific parts of the text could be selected for examining. Weaker answers also tend to list rather than engage in critical discussion.

A typical question might be 'Critically discuss the distinction that Descartes made between mind and body'.

Clearly the trigger demands more than just description of the arguments, so the evaluative skill will need to be demonstrated in order to score high marks. However, the arguments do need to be stated in reasonable detail as this aspect of the exam is focussed on a particular set text.

This type of question would feature as a part c) of a question and be worth 25 marks. This is worth more than parts a) and b) added together (20 marks). Often candidates spend far too long on questions worth only two or so marks and so penalise themselves.

Further Reading

R Audi *Epistemology* (Routledge, 1998)

A J Ayer *The Foundations of Empirical Knowledge* (Macmillan, 1940)

A J Ayer *Language, Truth and Logic* (Penguin, 1971, reprint)

A J Ayer, *The Problem of Knowledge* (Penguin, 1956)

S Bernecker (editor) *Knowledge:Readings in Contemporary Epistemology* (OUP, 2000)

S Blackburn *The Oxford Dictionary of Philosophy* (OUP, 1994)

P Carruthers *Introducing Persons* (Routledge, 1986)

J Cottingham *The Rationalists* (OUP, 1988)

E Craig *Knowledge and the State of Nature* (Oxford, 1990)

J Dancy *Introduction to Contemporary Epistemology* (Blackwell, 1985)

J Dancy (editor) *A Companion to Epistemology* (Blackwell, 1992)

B Davies *Thinking about God* (Chapman, 1985)

R Descartes *A Discourse on Method* (Everyman, 1995, reprint)

G Dicker *Descartes:An Analytical and Historical Introduction* (OUP, 1993)

W J Earle *Introduction to Philosophy* (McGraw-Hill, 1992)

S Evans *God, Reason and Theistic Proofs* (Edinburgh University Press, 1997)

E L Gettier *Is Justified True Belief Knowledge?* (Analysis 23:1967)

A Goldman *A Causal Theory of Knowing* (Journal of Philosophy, 64, 1978)

D Hamlyn *The Theory of Knowledge* (Macmillan, 1970)

T Honderich (editor) *The Oxford Companion to Philosophy* (OUP, 1995)

J Hospers *An Introduction to Philosophical Analysis* (Routledge, 1997, fourth edition)

D Hume *An Enquiry Concerning Human Understanding* (Oxford, 1995, reprint)

I Kant *Critique of Pure Reason* (Macmillan, 1961, reprint)

C Landesman *An Introduction to Epistemology* (Blackwell, 1997)

J Locke *Essay Concerning Human Understanding* (Dent, 1961, reprint)

E J Lowe *Locke on Human Understanding* (Routledge, 1995)

K Maslin *An Introduction to the Philosophy of Mind* (Polity, 2001)

A Morton *A Guide Through the Theory of Knowledge* (Blackwell, 1977)

T Nagel *The View from Nowhere* (Oxford, 1986)

R Osborne *Philosophy for Beginners* (Writers and Readers Publishing, 1992)

H Putman *Reason, Truth and History* (Cambridge, 1981)

B Russell *The Problems of Philosophy* (OUP, 1980, reprint)

R Scruton *Modern Philosophy* (Sinclair-Stevenson, 1994)

P Sloane *Test Your Lateral Thinking IQ* (Sterling, 1994)

R Solomon *The Big Questions* (Harcourt Brace, 1998, fifth edition)

L Wittgenstein *Philosophical Investigations* (Blackwell, 1953)

L Wittgenstein *Tractatus Logico-Philosophicus* (Routledge, 1961, reprint)

R S Woolhouse *The Empiricists* (OUP, 1988)

Index

a posteriori 17, 18, 25, 27, 35, 42
a priori 17, 18, 25, 28, 30, 31–2, 33, 42
analytic 27, 31, 35–6
anti-realism 7, 10, 55
Aquinas 10, 66
argument 1, 3, 4
Aristotle 9, 19, 20, 51, 78
assumptions 2
Ayer 11–12, 32, 59–60, 63, 64, 74

Berkeley 18, 27, 34, 61–2

Chomsky 29, 30, 35
cogito 17, 21–5, 33, 38
coherence 50, 53–4, 55
coherentism 43, 44–6, 48–9
correspondence 50, 51–3, 55
counterexample 7, 12–13, 15, 47
Craig 10, 14

deductive 1, 4,5
Descartes 9, 10, 17, 19–25, 28,
    29, 30, 33, 34, 38, 39, 58–9,
    66–8, 76, 77–84
dualism 77–84

empiricism 10, 27–34
epistemology 1, 2, 9–10
external world 65–72
externalism 14, 47
foundationalism 43, 44, 46, 48–9

Gettier 13, 16

Hume 10, 18, 27, 30, 34, 39–40,
    71, 72, 73, 74

idealism 61–3, 65
inductive 1, 4, 5
infinite regression 38, 44, 47
interactionism 77, 79, 80–3
internalism 14

justification 12–14, 15, 16, 43–9

Kant 10, 30–6, 69–70

language-games 50
lateral thinking 1, 3, 6
Leibniz 17, 21, 34
Locke 10, 18, 27, 28–9, 34, 58,
    60, 61, 62

Nagel 40
naïve realism 59–60, 64, 65
necessary condition 7, 11
Nozick 13–14

ontological 23, 33, 66, 67–71
perception 58–64
phenomenalism 63, 65
philosophical doubt 37, 39–40, 41, 42
Plato 9, 12, 18
pragmatism 50, 54, 55
primary qualities 57–8

rationalism 10, 17–26, 28, 31, 32, 35
realism 7, 10, 55
reliabilism 43, 44, 47, 48–9
representative realism 60–1, 64, 65
Russell 22, 23, 40, 69, 71–2, 73, 74, 76

scepticism 37–42
secondary qualities 57–8
Socrates 9, 18
solipsism 37, 40, 42
Spinoza 17
sufficient condition 7, 11
synthetic 27, 31, 35–6

theodicy 77, 82–3
trademark argument 66–7
truth 12, 14, 15, 16, 50–5

Wittgenstein 1, 41, 52

Zeno 17, 25